Newbery and Caldecott
Trivia and More for Every Day of the Year

NEWBERY AND CALDECOTT

TRIVIA AND MORE FOR EVERY DAY OF THE YEAR

Claudette Hegel

2000
Libraries Unlimited, Inc.
Englewood, Colorado

Libraries Unlimited, Inc.
P.O. Box 6633
Englewood, CO 80155-6633
1-800-237-6124
www.lu.com

Library of Congress Cataloging-in-Publication Data

Hegel, Claudette.
     Newbery and Caldecott trivia and more for every day of the year / Claudette Hegel.
          p. cm.
     Includes bibliographical references and indexes.
     ISBN 1-56308-830-4 (softbound)
       1. Newbery Medal. 2. Caldecott Medal. I. Title.

Z1037.A2 H44 2000
[PN1009.A1]
028.5′079--dc21

                                                        00-059352

CONTENTS

FOREWORD

by Dr. Deidre Johnson

"Only the rarest kind of best of anything
can be good enough for the young."
—Walter de la Mare

In the years since Frederic Melcher instituted the Newbery Award to heighten awareness of outstanding juvenile literature, children's books have become big business, resulting in a flood of available titles, everything from reprints of classics to some eminently missable—but heavily-marketed offerings. In recent years, children's books have also become a staple of most elementary school classrooms, where teachers face the problem of promoting the notable few amid the sea of lesser works. *Newbery and Caldecott Trivia and More for Every Day of the Year* offers valuable assistance to those wishing to introduce children to the best literature, for it highlights memorable works and their creators and, as an added bonus, provides glimpses into the history and eponymous figures behind the Newbery and Caldecott Awards.

Claudette Hegel's careful research into the background of Newbery and Caldecott Award winners and other notable children's books has produced a treasure trove of intriguing and illuminating information, designed to delight those already familiar with the works mentioned or pique the interest of those encountering the names of authors, illustrators, or titles for the first time. The format—one piece of trivia about a Newbery or Caldecott Award winner (or another significant work) for each day of the year, with

entries specifically keyed to birth dates of well-known authors and illustrators—extends the "calendar" approach by including tidbits that turn mere names into tantalizing people with human foibles, interests, and idiosyncrasies. There is rich material here for introducing books, promoting discussions of authors and ideas, designing creative writing assignments, or increasing understanding of the process of book creation and production. For example, the statement (January 3), "Chris Van Allsburg, who wrote and illustrated the book *Jumanji* about a board game coming to life, found board games disappointing as a child" offers a perfect prologue to reading *Jumanji*, a natural introduction to talk of how other dreary activities could be enlivened by the fantastic, or a potential springboard for examining how a creator's life experiences can be reapproached in fiction. Other entries, such as the many noting Newbery- and Caldecott-winning creators' fascination with earlier award winners, subtly reinforce ideas about the power of good literature and provide an inducement for additional reading.

The whole-language approach to reading encourages the use of children's literature to supplement every facet of the curriculum, from math to environmental awareness and multiculturalism, and the recent interest in reader-response criticism promotes personal connections with books. Both pedagogies are aided by numerous guides to juvenile fiction. While existing classroom-oriented supplements to children's literature may highlight notable books, their focus is often somewhat narrow— an examination of one title or genre rather than an awareness of books for multiple audiences and uses. *Newbery and Caldecott Trivia* takes a broader approach, recognizing the variety of literature used in the classroom—everything from the most recent award winners to nineteenth-century classics, and from picture books to young adult titles. In this, it reflects contemporary scholarship indicating that picture books are valuable not only for the primary grades but also for upper elementary students; it also recognized the diverse audiences and needs connected with children's literature: librarians who deal with children of all ages; teachers and home-schoolers who wish to draw upon the wide range of material available; substitute teachers who must be prepared to interest first-graders one day and fifth-graders another; parents in search of a book that can last through their children's different reading levels and interests. For those teachers using independent reading periods such as DEAR (Drop Everything And Read) or SST (Sustained Silent Reading), *Newbery and Caldecott Trivia* provides a wealth of tantalizing tidbits to intrigue a child looking for reading selections, allowing ample choice while still highlighting worthwhile literature.

Whether the book is used as a means of introducing notable names daily, as a source for looking up figures associated with particular days, or merely for casual browsing, there is something here for everyone. Like the awards Melcher instituted, *Newbery and Caldecott Trivia* provides a fine entrée into distinguished children's literature, an alluring enticement to experience and explore "the rarest kind of best."

INTRODUCTION

Authors and illustrators provide fascinating facts about themselves and their creations through lectures and writings, as well as through their biographical material. A list of references to these sources is provided for those who want to search for additional facts. The items of trivia included in the book have been selected for their educational value, humor, and simple appeal.

The trivia facts are arranged chronologically. Whenever possible, specific facts correspond with the subject's birthday, book publication date, or other pertinent date. Additional facts are scattered throughout the book. Each date includes at least one item about a Newbery Medal-winning book or author and a Caldecott Medal-winning book or illustrator. Some dates include information about a classic or popular book that didn't receive Newbery or Caldecott acclaim. Complete lists of Newbery and Caldecott books, through 2000, are provided in Appendixes A and B. The lists are arranged chronologically beginning with the year the American Library Association presented the first award: 1922 for the Newbery winners and 1938 for Caldecott winners. Separate indexes of people and titles are also included.

Many books that may have been worthy of Newbery and Caldecott acknowledgement were published before the inception of the awards or were simply overlooked by the selection committees. For that reason, it seems appropriate that those classic or popular books be included in the trivia facts.

Teachers often use these overlooked books—popular with children—in their classrooms through inclusion in a textbook, instead of a textbook, or simply as read-aloud books.

Knowing the background information about a book, an author, or an illustrator can encourage someone—adult or child—to read a particular book, whether the book didn't receive an award of any kind or was a Newbery or Caldecott winner.

The Newbery and Caldecott Awards

Each year, usually in late January or early February, the Association for Library Service to Children division of the American Library Association selects a book, considered to be the previous year's "most distinguished contribution to children's literature," on which to place the Newbery Medal. The Caldecott Medal is presented to the previous year's "most distinguished picture book." Other books also considered "distinguished" may be designated Honor Books, originally called Runners-up.

The author of the Newbery Medal book and the illustrator of the Caldecott Medal book receive a medal but no monetary prize, although any book that receives Newbery or Caldecott recognition shows a marked increase in sales. The medal is presented at an awards banquet held the following summer.

History of the Newbery and Caldecott Awards

Interest in children's books heightened after World War I. The Bookshop for Boys and Girls, the first bookstore stocking only children's books, opened in Boston in 1916. Three years later, Frederic Melcher, then editor of *Publishers Weekly*, organized the first Children's Book Week. Also in 1919, Macmillan became the first publisher with an editor who worked entirely with children's books.

This interest carried through the early 1920s. Members attending the 1921 American Library Association (ALA) Conference in Swampscott, Massachusetts, recognized this interest. Attendees discussed the excitement surrounding children's books.

Melcher thought a children's book award would help sustain that interest. During one of the sessions, he proposed an annual children's book award with funds he or his heirs would donate. Melcher suggested the award be named for John Newbery, the British publisher credited for publishing the first book intended solely for children's pleasure.

Initial response to the Newbery Medal was overwhelming, but after several years many thought the Newbery Committee overlooked books for younger children when making their selections.

Someone suggested another award for picture books. After much discussion, the Award Committee decided a new award wouldn't detract from the Newbery Medal. Melcher, agreeing to donate funds for a second award to be given to the illustrator of a picture book, suggested it be named for Randolph Caldecott, one of the best-known illustrators of the 1800s. The ALA passed a resolution for the Caldecott Medal on June 24, 1937.

The Newbery and Caldecott Medals have become two of the most prestigious awards in children's literature. The Medals have helped many teachers, librarians, publishers, authors, illustrators, and even those not associated with the book business become more interested in children's literature.

The Newbery and Caldecott Selection Process

Originally, the Newbery Award was selected primarily by popular vote, but within a few years a committee was established. Members of the committee, some elected and some appointed, must be members of the ALA's Association for Library Service to Children (ALSC).

Details of the actual process of selecting a winning book change with each Newbery Committee and Caldecott Committee. Whatever process is used, members of the committee must read many books, keep up with much correspondence over a year, and spend many hours in meetings to select the winners.

The committee must be certain the books considered for the Newbery or Caldecott Award meet certain qualifications. Some of the requirements are:

- The book must be "marked by eminence and distinction: noted for significant achievement."

- The author(s) [for Newbery] or illustrator(s) [for Caldecott] must reside in or be a citizen of the United States.

- The work must be original; reprints are not acceptable. Retellings of traditional tales are acceptable.

- The work must not be a compilation.

- The work must be published in the United States.

- A book must be copyrighted in the preceding year (e.g., only a book with a copyright of 2000 would be eligible for the 2001 Medal).

- Children must be the intended audience for the book.

- The book must be a "self-contained entity" (meaning no book with sound, video, or any other device needed for the book's enjoyment can be considered).

Copies of the Newbery Award and Caldecott Award criteria are available from the American Library Association. Mail your request, with a self-addressed, stamped, business-sized envelope, to Association for Library Service to Children, American Library Association, 50 East Huron Street, Chicago, IL 60611.

About John Newbery

Oliver Goldsmith in *Vicar of Wakefield* describes the character based on John Newbery as "the philanthropic bookseller of St. Paul's Churchyard, who has written so many books for children, calling himself their friend, but who was the friend of all mankind." Newbery encouraged his friend Goldsmith to write first for magazines, then later children's books, possibly even some that Newbery published. Newbery often helped his friends both by encouraging their work and by giving them money.

Dr. Samuel Johnson, another of Newbery's friends, called him Jack Whirler in the *Idler*. Johnson said when Jack Whirler "enters a house his first declaration is that he cannot sit down, and so short are his visits that he seldom appears to have come for any reason but to say he must go." Newbery, an avid reader and writer, may have been in a hurry to get back to his books. Johnson also said that he didn't know which Newbery did more of: read books or write them.

John Newbery was born in 1713 in Waltham St. Lawrence, Berkshire, England. He was largely self-taught because the family had little money for education. In 1730, he moved to Reading, England, where he worked on a provincial newspaper owned by William Carnan. Newbery must have been valued as a worker because he inherited a part of the estate when Carnan died in 1737. Newbery later married Carnan's widow.

Newbery spent some time touring England before he founded his publishing house in 1740. He moved to London in 1744 or 1745, where he finally settled at St. Paul's Churchyard in a location he described as "over against the north door of the Cathedral."

To earn a living, Newbery carried a variety of items in his shop called the "Bible and Sun." In addition to books, he sold haberdashery, cutlery, gingerbread, and nostrums and remedies such as Cephalic Snuff, Dr. Hooper's Female Pills, and Dr. James's Fever Powder.

An astute businessman, Newbery noticed the success of *The Child's New Plaything*, a book published in 1743 and dedicated to the young Prince George. The title page of this spelling book said it was intended "to make the Learning to Read a Diversion instead of a Task."

Newbery published *A Little Pretty Pocket-Book* in 1744. The book, consisting of fables, jingles, and games, was primarily for children to read for fun instead of as a method of learning. His advertisements for the book said, "The books are given away only the binding to be paid for." The cost per book was sixpence alone, but eightpence with a "Ball or Pincushion."

The book's success led him to begin *The Lilliputian Magazine or The Young Gentleman's and Lady's Golden Library*, possibly the first magazine for children. The magazine contained stories, games, jokes, and riddles, as well as advertising. Newbery described the magazine as "an Attempt to mend the World, to render the society of Man more Amiable and to Establish the Plainness, Simplicity, Virtue and Wisdom of the Golden Age . . . Printed for the Society . . . at Mr. Newbery's, the Bible and Sun, in St. Paul's Churchyard."

Newbery designed and produced a total of about thirty books for children. He always made sure his books had a moral in them, so parents would buy them. All of his books were issued anonymously or under alliterative pseudonyms such as Abraham Aesop and Tommy Trapwit.

Books written by others that Newbery published consisted of alphabet books, collections of fables and poems, novels, histories, riddle books, science books, and possibly the first encyclopedia for children—the ten-volume *The Circle of Sciences.* Newbery's books were characterized by being lighthearted, energetic, humorous, and physically well-made.

After Newbery's death on December 22, 1767, his son and nephew—both named Francis Newbery—continued his work. The nephew's widow, Elizabeth, operated the business from 1769–1801. In 1801, John Harris took over the business and continued publishing for children. His family's respect for Newbery is evident: Harris's grandson is named "John Newbery Harris."

Newbery believed that books were a means of influencing children to be good. In *Tom Telescope,* he said books should represent to children "their Duties and future Interests in a Manner that shall seem rather intended to amuse than instruct."

Between 1740 and 1815, Newbery's firm published about 2,400 books. Approximately 400 of those books were for children, but those 400 children's books are for what John Newbery is best remembered.

About Randolph Caldecott

Randolph Caldecott is known for breaking the rules of illustrating for children and establishing new ones. He had high standards of technical excellence, detail, beauty, and humor and had insight in both the foregrounds and backgrounds of his illustrations.

Randolph Caldecott was born on Bridge Street in the town of Chester in Cheshire, England on March 22, 1846. Randolph, his parents (John and Mary Dinah Brookes Caldecott), and his brother Alfred lived above a shop where John Caldecott was a woolen draper, tailor, and hatter. In August of 1852, when Randolph was only six years old, his mother died of a fever.

Randolph, himself, had rheumatic fever as a child. The illness left him "delicate" the rest of his life; heart trouble and gastritis limited his activities. Luckily, Randolph didn't let his illness limit him too much. His good humor is evident in a letter he wrote to a friend saying, "Consumption be damned! It is consumption of cigarettes and Chianti that interests me."

Randolph started drawing almost as soon as he could hold a pencil. By the age of six, he was drawing pictures of animals, then modeling them in clay or cutting them out of wood. His physical weakness may have increased his interest in art because he wasn't able to take part in many athletic activities.

Randolph Caldecott attended the Chester School of Art and King's School, which was attached to the Chester Cathedral. Later, he took a class taught by the English painter Sir Edward J. Poynter. His classmates included James Whistler, Thomas Lamont, and Sir John Gilbert.

Because his father didn't encourage his artistic talents, the fifteen-year-old Randolph Caldecott moved to Whitchurch, Shropshire, to become a clerk with the Whitchurch and Ellesmere Bank. As a sideline, he tried to sell life insurance, but failed to sell even one policy.

As an adult, Randolph Caldecott was described as having a gentle voice, a quiet manner, compassion, and great humor. As far as his physical appearance, a friend described Caldecott by saying, "The handsome lad carried his own recommendation. With light-brown hair falling with a ripple over his brow, blue-gray eyes shaded with long lashes, sweet and mobile mouth, tall and well-made—he joined to these physical advantages a gay good humor and charming disposition."

Caldecott especially loved the outdoors. Wherever he lived, he roamed the streets and countryside making sketches of his surroundings. Many of the things he sketched later appeared in his published drawings, some of which can be recognized even today. Most of the sketches of himself show him with a beard because that was the style at the time.

Randolph Caldecott didn't correct details on illustrations he found unsatisfactory. If a sketch didn't turn out right, he simply discarded it and started a new one. He used many of these imperfect sketches as protective wrapping for his packages and letters.

On December 7, 1861, the *Illustrated London News* carried Caldecott's first published work. The newspaper printed his drawing of a fire that had destroyed the Queen Hotel on City Road. He hadn't bothered to sign the drawing because he didn't think it would be published.

In 1867, Caldecott moved to Manchester where he worked at the Manchester and Salford Bank. While there, he joined the Brasenose Club and studied in the Manchester School of Art. Soon, local weeklies published his illustrations and galleries exhibited his paintings.

Caldecott moved to London in 1872 after Henry Blackburn, editor of the magazine *London Society*, bought several of his drawings. Blackburn urged Caldecott to become a book illustrator because he thought the pressures of illustrating for magazines and newspapers would worsen the artist's already poor health.

In January 1877, after illustrating first several travel books, then other books, Caldecott moved to the French Riviera for his health. By that time Edmund Evans, a wood engraver and color printer, had begun to see a rising interest in children's books. He contacted Caldecott, and they collaborated on sixteen shilling toy books, two published each year at Christmas between 1878 and 1885. The first two books sold so well that the initial printings for the next books were 100,000 each. Eventually the books were bound, four to a volume, with board covers.

In 1879, Caldecott bought a country house in Kemsing, a small village near Sevenoaks in Kent, England. While living at that home (Wybournes), he courted and married Marian H. Brind. Caldecott was thirty-three when he married. Three years later, the couple moved to London and also bought a country home in Farnham, Surrey. The Caldecotts usually wintered in the South of France to escape England's dampness.

In 1885, the Caldecotts traveled to the United States where Randolph could find new scenes to sketch. They docked in New York in October, traveled to Philadelphia, and continued down the East Coast. They planned to spend the winter in Florida, then travel to Colorado and California and finish their trip in Boston.

The stress of traveling, combined with one of Florida's coldest winters on record, worsened Caldecott's poor health. On February 13, 1886, Randolph Caldecott died of "organic disease of the heart" in St. Augustine, Florida. His body is buried in Evergreen Cemetery in St. Augustine. Marian Caldecott died in 1932, forty-six years after her husband. The couple had no children.

Although much of Randolph Caldecott's fine art and illustrations were intended for adults, he will be best remembered for his unique free-spirited style of illustrating for children.

January 1

The Story of Mankind, written and illustrated by Hendrik Van Loon, received the first Newbery Medal in 1922.

Animals of the Bible, illustrated by Dorothy Lathrop and text selected by Helen Dean Fish, received the first Caldecott Medal in 1938.

The only monetary prize for the Newbery and Caldecott Medals is the increase in sales of the winning books due to the publicity generated by the awards.

January 2

A Visit to William Blake's Inn, written by Nancy Willard and illustrated by Alice Provensen and Martin Provensen, is the first and only book so far to be selected by both the Newbery (1982 Newbery Medal) and Caldecott (1982 Honor Book) Committees.

Leo Dillon and Diane Dillon spent three months researching the illustrations for *Ashanti to Zulu: African Traditions* (1977 Caldecott Medal), but only one month actually creating the illustrations.

Louisa May Alcott's working title for *Little Women* was "The Pathetic Family."

January 3

 BORN ON THIS DAY:
J. R. R. Tolkien, 1892

Much of Virginia Sorensen's (*Miracles on Maple Hill*, 1957 Newbery Medal) writing was done at her dining room table with a dog lying at her feet. For a few weeks, kittens lived on the table where she worked.

Chris Van Allsburg, who wrote and illustrated the book *Jumanji* (1982 Caldecott Medal) about a board game coming to life, found board games disappointing as a child.

J. J. R. Tolkien wrote much of *The Lord of the Rings* on the backs of undergraduates' exam papers during a wartime paper shortage.

January 4

 BORN ON THIS DAY:
Jacob Grimm, 1785
Phyllis Reynolds Naylor, 1933

Jon Lanman, the editor of *Shiloh* (1992 Newbery Medal), included his dog's pawprint next to his signature on his acceptance letter to Phyllis Reynolds Naylor. He wrote, "Lucy, my eleven-year-old Labrador, salutes you!"

Rika Lesser, who retold *Hansel and Gretel* (1985 Caldecott Honor Book), helped the book's illustrator, Paul Zelinsky, write the text of *Rapunzel* (1998 Caldecott Medal).

Jacob Grimm and Wilhelm Grimm didn't intend the audience for their fairy tales to be children. They wrote the tales as part of a scholarly study on the history of the German language and oral traditions.

January 5

Ruth Sawyer said she had very little to do with the writing of *Roller Skates* (1937 Newbery Medal). She claimed that editor May Massee simply made a book out of Lucinda's story.

Rachel Field wrote *Prayer for a Child* (1945 Caldecott Medal) for her daughter, Hannah.

Alexandre Dumas, author of *The Three Musketeers*, fought his first duel on January 5, 1825, at the age of 23. His pants fell down during the course of the duel.

January 6

Sharon Creech ended her acceptance speech for *Walk Two Moons* (1995 Newbery Medal) the way the book ends: "Huzza, Huzza!"

McElligot's Pool by Dr. Seuss (1948 Caldecott Honor Book) impressed first-grader David Wisniewski (*Golem*, 1997 Caldecott Medal).

L. Frank Baum's original title for *The Wizard of Oz* was "The Emerald City." Because of a superstition that publishing a book with a jewel in the title was unlucky, the title was changed.

January 7

Garth Williams's first attempts to illustrate *Charlotte's Web* (1953 Newbery Honor Book) showed the spider with a woman's face. Because author E. B. White wanted body positions, not facial expressions, to reflect the characters' feelings, he sent Williams books about spiders to help him make the drawings more realistic.

Fenton Newbery, great-grandson of John Newbery, attended the Newbery Award Ceremony in 1926.

Ludwig Bemelmans paid the daughters of Phyllis McGinley (*All Around the Town*, 1949 Caldecott Honor Book; *The Most Wonderful Doll in the World*, 1951 Caldecott Honor Book) fifty cents each for their idea to include a dog in the next book about Madeline. That book, *Madeline's Rescue*, received the 1954 Caldecott Medal.

Ann M. Martin originally intended the Baby-Sitters Club series to stop after four books.

January 8

 BORN ON THIS DAY:
Nancy Bond, 1945
Sorche Nic Leodhas, 1898

When Nancy Bond saw her "tattered, corrected" manuscript pages as the book *A String in the Harp* (1977 Newbery Honor Book), she realized she hadn't only completed a book, but she had also started her career as writer.

Librarian Leclaire Gowans Hoffman Alger wrote under the name Sorche Nic Leodhas (*Always Room for One More*, 1966 Caldecott Medal).

In the final poem of Lewis Carroll's *Through the Looking Glass*, the name Alice Pleasance Liddell is spelled out with the first letter of each line. Alice Liddell was the girl for whom the book's main character was named.

January 9

The first balloon ascension took place on this day in 1793. William Pène du Bois (*The Twenty-One Balloons*, 1948 Newbery Medal) collected model balloons.

Emily Arnold McCully based Mirette's characterization in *Mirette on the High Wire* (1993 Caldecott Medal) on photographs of the author Colette as a child.

Charles Dickens used an actual inn called the George and Vulture as a meeting place for his characters in *The Pickwick Papers*. Today, the Pickwick Club uses that same building for meetings.

January 10

Karen Hesse kept a picture of Lucille Burroughs (photographed by Walker Evans) near her while writing *Out of the Dust* (1998 Newbery Medal). By coincidence, her editor selected the same photograph for the book jacket.

Cynthia Rylant wrote *When I Was Young in the Mountains* (1983 Caldecott Honor Book) as a tribute to her grandparents.

Kenneth Grahame told his son, nicknamed Mouse, stories every day. When Mouse refused to go on a trip because he didn't want to miss the stories, his father promised to send him a story every day. Seeing the value in the stories, Mouse's governess saved them. Those stories became the basis for the book *The Wind in the Willows*.

January 11

BORN ON THIS DAY:
Robert C. O'Brien, 1918

Robert C. O'Brien (*Mrs. Frisby and the Rats of NIMH*, 1972 Newbery Medal) was the pseudonym of Robert Leslie Conly. He had to write under a pen name because his employer, *National Geographic*, didn't want their writers working for anyone else.

Harcourt publishers organized a cocktail party celebrating the 1952 Newbery and Caldecott Medalists, author Eleanor Estes (*Ginger Pye*) and illustrator Nicolas Mordvinoff (*Finders Keepers*). When Mordvinoff failed to appear at a dinner following the party, Estes feared he disliked her, but he'd simply left with another woman he met at the party.

The character of Peter Pan first appeared as a baby in a section of J. M. Barrie's book *The Little White Bird*, published in 1902.

January 12

BORN ON THIS DAY:
Laura Adams Armer, 1874
Jack London, 1876
Charles Perrault, 1628

Longman Publishers sponsored a writing contest in which Laura Adams Armer won first place for her manuscript which became the book *Waterless Mountain* (1932 Newbery Medal).

The many folk and fairy tales collected under the name Charles Perrault, author of *Cinderella* (1955 Caldecott Medal), may have actually been written by Pierre Perrault, Charles's father, who simply gave his son the credit.

Jack London left home at age fifteen to become a sailor. He lived many of the adventures he used as a basis for his books.

January 13

BORN ON THIS DAY:
Michael Bond, 1926

Home and family were the only things more important than writing in the life of Elizabeth George Speare (*The Witch of Blackbird Pond*, 1959 Newbery Medal, and *The Bronze Bow*, 1962 Newbery Medal).

A 1976 *Publishers Weekly* survey shows that people in the children's book field consider *Where the Wild Things Are* (1964 Caldecott Medal) the second best children's book written in America.

The original Paddington was a tiny toy bear that Michael Bond found on a shelf in London. Because all of the other bears had been sold, Bond bought the toy for his wife. They named the bear after Paddington Station, located near their home.

January 14

 BORN ON THIS DAY:

Thornton W. Burgess, 1874

Hugh Lofting, 1886

Hendrik Van Loon, 1882

The first and second Newbery Medalists, Hendrik Van Loon (*The Story of Mankind*, 1922) and Hugh Lofting (*The Voyages of Doctor Dolittle*, 1923), shared the same birthday, being born just four years apart. The third Newbery Medalist, Charles Boardman Hawes (*The Dark Frigate*, 1924) was also born in January, on the 24th.

The border pattern on *The Little House* (1943 Caldecott Medal) endpapers represents the history of transportation.

Thornton W. Burgess's animal books sold well over eight million copies by 1955.

January 15

Madeleine L'Engle (*A Wrinkle in Time*, 1963 Newbery Medal) wrote her first story at the age of six. The story concerned a little "grul" [girl] who lived in a cloud.

Robert McCloskey was the first person to receive two Caldecott Medals: *Make Way for Ducklings* in 1942 and *Time of Wonder* in 1958. So far, only Marcia Brown has received three Caldecott Medals.

Frances Hodgson Burnett's *Little Lord Fauntleroy* is on a list of the 100 most influential books.

January 16

Lois Lowry's friend suggested that Lowry change a dessert from "apple pie" to "applesauce" in *Number the Stars* (1990 Newbery Medal) because apple pie was rare in Denmark during World War II.

When Lynd Ward (*The Biggest Bear*, 1953 Caldecott Medal) was in the first grade, he realized his last name was "draw" spelled backward.

Roald Dahl, author of *Charlie and the Chocolate Factory* and other books, was married to actress Patricia Neal.

January 17

When she gave the manuscript for *The Westing Game* (1979 Newbery Medal) to her editor, Ellen Raskin said, "This is definitely *not* a Newbery Medal book. It's too much fun."

As a child, Verna Aardema (*Why Mosquitoes Buzz in People's Ears*, 1976 Caldecott Medal) often went to a swamp to think up stories—and as a way to get out of household chores.

Harper Lee based the boy Dill in *To Kill a Mockingbird* on the boy who lived next door to her when she was growing up. That boy was future author Truman Capote.

January 18

 BORN ON THIS DAY:

A. A. Milne, 1882

Arthur Ransome, 1884

When Elizabeth Lewis (*Young Fu of the Upper Yangtze*, 1933 Newbery Medal) was born, the nurse told her mother that Elizabeth would spend her life in two countries—and she did: China and the United States.

Arthur Ransome's (*The Fool of the World and the Flying Ship*, 1969 Caldecott Medal) varied jobs included working as a newspaper correspondent, a fisherman, and a ghost writer for famous sportsmen.

A. A. Milne based Winnie-the-Pooh on a stuffed bear owned by his son, Christopher Robin.

January 19

 BORN ON THIS DAY:
Edgar Allan Poe, 1809

E. B. White completed the first draft of *Charlotte's Web* (1953 Newbery Honor Book) on January 19, 1951. He had begun writing the manuscript in longhand about two years earlier.

Jerry Pinkney had trouble deciding how to illustrate Brother Wind in *Mirandy and Brother Wind* (1989 Caldecott Honor Book), despite the fact that he had a clear picture of the rest of the book very quickly.

If Edgar Allan Poe had been a girl, he would have been named "Cordelia" for the character his actress mother portrayed in *King Lear*. Because Poe's actor father portrayed the villain Edmund, they named the baby "Edgar" after Edmund's brother.

January 20

Charles G. Waugh and Martin H. Greenberg collected short stories from eighteen Newbery winners and compiled them into *The*

Newbery Award Reader published by Harcourt Brace Jovanovich in 1984.

Ed Young's *Lon Po Po* (1990 Caldecott Medal) and Trina Schart Hyman's *Little Red Riding Hood* (1984 Caldecott Honor Book) are both versions of the same story.

A Swedish publishing house awarded first prize in a writing contest to Astrid Lindgren for her story about Pippi Longstocking.

January 21

About thirty of Mildred Taylor's friends and relatives attended the 1977 Awards Banquet when she accepted the Newbery Medal for *Roll of Thunder, Hear My Cry*. Normally, only two guests of the author are present.

Barbara Cooney followed the route the ox-cart man took as research for *Ox-Cart Man* (1980 Caldecott Medal). She decided to use 1832 for the setting because she wanted to draw a man with a beard and beards were popular between 1803 and 1847.

Rudyard Kipling's *Kim* is ranked seventy-eighth on The Modern Library Board's List of the 100 Best Novels Published in the English Language since 1900.

January 22

 BORN ON THIS DAY:
Blair Lent, 1930

The Story of Mankind (1922 Newbery Medal) likely netted Hendrik Van Loon over a half of a million dollars—equivalent to several million dollars today.

Blair Lent (*The Funny Little Woman*, 1973 Caldecott Medal) used his increased income after winning the Caldecott Medal to move from the city to the country.

Although John Newbery is often credited with publishing the first Mother Goose book in London in 1760, Thomas Fleet printed *Mother Goose's Melodies* in Boston in 1719. Fleet's mother-in-law, Elizabeth Goose, wrote the book using some verses she remembered and some she wrote herself.

January 23

On the night of the Newbery and Caldecott Awards Banquet, Monica Shannon (*Dobry*, 1935 Newbery Medal) accidentally put her dress on backward and had to reverse it in the taxi on the way to the ceremony.

David Macaulay (*Black and White*, 1991 Newbery Medal) completed his first successful drawing when he was eight years old. It was of a fire engine.

Copies of Mark Twain's *The Adventures of Tom Sawyer* sold very slowly right after the book was published.

January 24

 BORN ON THIS DAY:
Charles Boardman Hawes, 1889

Charles Boardman Hawes died at age 34, just before *The Dark Frigate* (1924 Newbery Medal) was published. His wife accepted the award for him. So far, Hawes is the only person to receive a Newbery Medal posthumously.

John Schoenherr read Jane Yolen's manuscript for *Owl Moon* (1988 Caldecott Medal) with the intention of sending it back to the editor saying he wouldn't illustrate it. Luckily, he read the manuscript a second time and changed his mind.

Bruce Coville, author of *My Teacher Is an Alien* and many other books, worked as a cookware salesman, assembly line worker, toy maker, grave digger, and elementary school teacher before he began a career as a writer.

January 25

Beverly Cleary (*Dear Mr. Henshaw*, 1984 Newbery Medal) wrote novelizations of the *Leave It To Beaver* television series.

Katherine Paterson received a letter from a teacher thanking her for making Gilly in *The Great Gilly Hopkins* (1979 Newbery Honor Book) such a good role model. Paterson doesn't think someone who cheats, lies, and steals is a good role model.

Margot Zemach wanted to make the devil in *Duffy and the Devil* (1974 Caldecott Medal) more lewd, but she changed her mind when she heard about people painting diapers on the boy in the 1971 Caldecott Honor Book *In the Night Kitchen*.

January 26

 BORN ON THIS DAY:
Mary Mapes Dodge, 1831

Jane Leslie Conly (*Crazy Lady!*, 1994 Newbery Honor Book) finished *Z for Zachariah* at the request of her father, Robert C. O'Brien (*Mrs. Frisby and the Rats of NIMH*, 1972 Newbery Medal), who knew he would die soon. Conly's mother edited the manuscript.

Ezra Jack Keats (*The Snowy Day*, 1963 Caldecott Medal) grew up in a tough neighborhood. A gang once ordered him to give them a picture he'd drawn. They admired it, then returned the drawing to Keats.

Mary Mapes Dodge, author of *Hans Brinker, or, The Silver Skates*, didn't visit the Netherlands until several years after she had written the book set in Holland.

January 27

 BORN ON THIS DAY:
Lewis Carroll, 1832
Julius Lester, 1939

As a child, Donna Diamond, illustrator of *Bridge to Terabithia* (1978 Newbery Medal), enjoyed *Alice's Adventures in Wonderland*. Her illustrations helped *Bridge to Terabithia* win the 1978 Lewis Carroll Shelf Award.

Jerry Pinkney wanted to illustrate a book about John Henry, and he asked Julius Lester to write the story. *John Henry* became a Caldecott Honor Book in 1995.

The Lewis Carroll Shelf award is presented to books worthy of sitting on a shelf next to the books by Lewis Carroll.

January 28

 BORN ON THIS DAY:
Vera Williams, 1927

Paul Fleischman (*Joyful Noise*, 1989 Newbery Medal) grew up listening to his father, Sid Fleischman (*The Whipping Boy*, 1987 Newbery Medal) read his books-in-progress to the family.

Vera Williams's love for a new grandchild inspired *"More More More," Said the Baby* (1991 Caldecott Honor Book).

Laura Ingalls Wilder's first book, *Little House in the Big Woods*, was published when she was 65 years old.

January 29

Doris Gates got the idea for *Blue Willow* (1941 Newbery Honor Book) from her experiences as a librarian helping hundreds of children from migrant worker families.

Soon after completing *Chanticleer and the Fox* (1959 Caldecott Medal), Barbara Cooney found herself shaping the characters from the book out of gingerbread to use as ornaments on the Christmas tree.

Edgar Allan Poe's poem "The Raven" first appeared in the New York *Evening Mirror* on January 29, 1845.

January 30

 BORN ON THIS DAY:
Lloyd Alexander, 1924

Lloyd Alexander (*The High King*, 1969 Newbery Medal) was once a member of the United States Army Intelligence.

Ed Emberly used only three colors—red, yellow, and blue—in creating the illustrations for *Drummer Hoff* (1968 Caldecott Medal). The other ten colors in the book are combinations of these three primary colors.

Margery Bianco always wanted to write about her toys. She had a rabbit named Fluffy that became the basis for *The Velveteen Rabbit*.

January 31

A twelve-year-old boy wrote to Elizabeth Yates (*Amos Fortune, Free Man*, 1951 Newbery Medal) and said, "Amos Fortune must have been a great guy. Did you know him?" Yates felt that she did.

Illustrator Mary Azarian learned that her book *Snowflake Bentley* had won the 1999 Caldecott Medal minutes after helping a friend dig out her car, which was stuck in the snow.

In response to criticism that his "wild things" are too scary, Maurice Sendak (*Where the Wild Things Are*, 1964 Caldecott Medal) said that children had sent him their versions of what "wild things" look like. He said some of their illustrations made his "wild things" look like "cuddly fuzzballs."

The Yearling by Marjorie Kinnan Rawlings was the best-selling book of fiction in 1938 and the seventh best-selling book of fiction in 1939.

February 1

 BORN ON THIS DAY:
Jerry Spinelli, 1941

When his hometown librarian asked Jerry Spinelli (*Maniac Magee*, 1991 Newbery Medal) if he was a "maniac," he answered, "I sure am. Aren't we all?"

Roger Duvoisin was surprised that *White Snow, Bright Snow* won the 1948 Caldecott Medal. He thought people would have been tired of snow after the harsh winter they'd just had.

As a child, Lewis Carroll's hobbies were performing magic tricks and practicing puppetry.

February 2

Few young readers have complained about the ending in *Jacob Have I Loved* (1981 Newbery Medal), but many adult critics have said the book ends too suddenly.

Some of the people involved in the film version of *Zlateh the Goat* (1967 Newbery Honor Book) didn't trust Maurice Sendak's research in illustrating the book. The filmmakers checked to see if a nanny goat can have horns or if only billy goats have horns. Sendak was right: nanny goats can have horns.

Trina Schart Hyman (*Saint George and the Dragon*, 1985 Caldecott Medal) couldn't bring herself to draw the scene of George actually killing the dragon. She called author Margaret Hodges who suggested Hyman simply show the scene *after* Saint George killed the dragon.

February 3

As a child, Joan Blos's (*A Gathering of Days*, 1980 Newbery Medal) favorite books were all Newbery Award-winners: *Caddie Woodlawn* (1936), *The Trumpeter of Krakow* (1929), *Roller Skates* (1937), and *Hitty: Her First Hundred Years* (1930).

Wanda Gág's *Snow White and the Seven Dwarfs* (1939 Caldecott Honor Book) and Randall Jarell's *Snow-White and the Seven Dwarfs*, illustrated by Nancy Ekholm Burkert (1973 Caldecott Honor Book), are both versions of the same story.

Of *Adventures of Huckleberry Finn*, Ernest Hemingway said, "The best book we've had. All American writing comes from that. There was nothing before. There has been nothing as good since."

February 4

Robert Lawson pointed out that rabbits had a good year in the arts in 1945. That year, Lawson's *Rabbit Hill* won the Newbery Award, and the play *Harvey*, written by Mary Chase, received the Pulitzer Prize.

A picture of a ragged girl in Evaline Ness's portfolio became the inspiration for Sam in *Sam, Bangs and Moonshine* (1967 Caldecott Medal). Ness added Bangs because her own cat sat on her artwork and ate her erasers. The "moonshine" is because Evaline fibbed a lot when she was a child.

When *Robinson Crusoe* was published in 1719, the full title was *The Life and Strange Surprising Adventures of Robinson Crusoe*.

February 5

 BORN ON THIS DAY:
David Wiesner, 1956

Jean Craighead George's son had read all the Newbery books at the time his mother won the Newbery Award for *Julie of the Wolves* in 1973.

David Wiesner (*Tuesday*, 1992 Caldecott Medal) spent most of his childhood drawing.

The character Curious George originally appeared in the French book *Cecily G. and the Nine Monkeys*.

February 6

Karen Cushman (*The Midwife's Apprentice*, 1996 Newbery Medal) saw the phrase "midwife's apprentice" and built the book around it.

Barbara Cooney questioned whether she was really in the career meant for her until after *Ox-Cart Man* won the Caldecott Award in 1980.

A governess named Miss Hammond encouraged Beatrix Potter to draw and also helped develop her interest in natural history.

February 7

 BORN ON THIS DAY:
Jean Charlot, 1898
Charles Dickens, 1812
Helen Dean Fish, 1889
Fred Gipson, 1908
Laura Ingalls Wilder, 1867

Fred Gipson said he thought every school child in America wrote a fan letter to him after *Old Yeller* (1957 Newbery Honor Book) was published.

Laura Ingalls Wilder, author of several Newbery Honor Books, was the recipient of the first Laura Ingalls Wilder award in 1954. The award is given to an author or illustrator in recognition of an entire body of work.

Jean Charlot (illustrator of *Secret of the Andes*, 1953 Newbery Medal; *And Now Miguel*, 1954 Newbery Medal; *A Child's Good Night Book*, 1944 Caldecott Honor Book; and *When Will the World Be Mine?*, 1954 Caldecott Honor Book) is of Mexican descent on his mother's side, but didn't visit Mexico until he was in his twenties.

Helen Dean Fish (*Animals of the Bible*, 1938 Caldecott Medal) was the third full-time children's book editor in history.

Charles Dickens wrote an average of 2,000 words per day.

February 8

 BORN ON THIS DAY:
Jules Verne, 1828

As a child, Elizabeth Borton de Treviño (*I, Juan de Pareja*, 1966 Newbery Medal) never wanted to put her books aside to set the table, dust, or do other chores. Her favorite reward was to be allowed to go to the library.

While researching *Make Way for Ducklings* (1942 Caldecott Medal), Robert McCloskey visited the Natural History Museum in New York to learn all he could about ducks, from how they looked to how they had changed along the evolutionary scale.

Jules Verne, author of *20,000 Leagues Under the Sea*, ran away from home and boarded a ship at age eleven, but he returned home the first time the ship docked.

February 9

When Julius Lester learned *To Be a Slave* was named a Newbery Honor Book in 1969, his first question was "What's that?" He then asked, "Any money?" He hung up as soon as he learned no money was involved.

At age twelve, Marcia Brown surprised her librarian by spending her time studying picture books. When the librarian learned of Brown's interest in art, she let her enter the closed stacks where art books for adults were located. Brown went on to illustrate three Caldecott Medal-winning books and six Caldecott Honor Books.

Nathaniel Hawthorne washed his hands before opening a letter from his wife Sophie to prevent contaminating anything she had touched.

February 10

 BORN ON THIS DAY:
Stephen Gammell, 1943
E. L. Konigsburg, 1930

In 1968, E. L. Konigsburg became the only person so far to receive both the top Newbery Award (*From the Mixed-up Files of Mrs. Basil E. Frankweiler*) and a Newbery Honor Book Award (*Jennifer, Hecate, Macbeth, William McKinley, and Me, Elizabeth*) in the same year.

In one illustration in *Song and Dance Man* (1989 Caldecott Medal), the stripes on Grandpa's vest run horizontal instead of vertical as they do in the other illustrations.

Illustrator Stephen Gammell wanted to see if anyone would notice.

A 1976 *Publishers Weekly* survey of teachers, librarians, publishers, and authors indicated that *Little Women* was the fourth best children's book written in America.

February 11

 BORN ON THIS DAY:
Jane Yolen, 1939

Whenever Dhan Mukerji (*Gay-Neck, the Story of a Pigeon*, 1928 Newbery Medal) spoke, he always seemed to end up talking about the jungles of India, no matter what the topic was when he started.

Jane Yolen wrote *Owl Moon* (1988 Caldecott Medal) as a love letter to her family.

Many publishers rejected the manuscript for George Orwell's *Animal Farm*, fearing that the political aspects of the story would create problems for the company.

February 12

 BORN ON THIS DAY:
Judy Blume, 1938

Biographies of Abraham Lincoln won both the Newbery Medal (*Lincoln: A Photobiography*, 1988) and the Caldecott Medal (*Abraham Lincoln*, 1940). Two Newbery Honor Books also discuss Lincoln's life (*Abraham Lincoln's World*, 1945; *Abraham Lincoln, Friend of the People*, 1951).

In 1952, both the top Newbery book and the top Caldecott book were about dogs: *Ginger Pye* (Newbery Medal) and *Finders Keepers* (Caldecott Medal).

Judy Blume's books rarely appear on awards lists when the winners are selected by adults, but book awards chosen by children frequently include Blume's books.

February 13

 BORN ON THIS DAY:

Janet Taylor Lisle, 1947
William Sleator, 1945

While in college, Janet Taylor Lisle (*Afternoon of the Elves*, 1990 Newbery Honor Book) participated in several protest marches, strikes, and debates but often found herself beginning to see the opposition's point-of-view.

William Sleator (*The Angry Moon*, 1971 Caldecott Honor Book) wrote the musical score for the animated version of *Why the Sun and Moon Live in the Sky* (1969 Caldecott Honor Book).

A whaling ship named *Essex* was sunk by a sperm whale in 1820. Herman Melville, author of *Moby Dick*, heard about the adventures aboard the ship directly from the ship's first mate.

February 14

 BORN ON THIS DAY:

Jamake Highwater, 1942
Paul O. Zelinsky, 1953

Jamake Highwater (*Anpao: An American Indian Odyssey*, 1978 Newbery Honor Book) was a stuntman in movie westerns. He said he "died hundreds of times for John Wayne."

"Paul Oser Zelinsky" (*Rapunzel*, 1998 Caldecott Medal) is an anagram for "Rapunzel's key oils."

In 1931, China banned *Alice's Adventures in Wonderland* because "animals should not use human language," and it was "disastrous to put animals and human beings on the same level."

February 15

Hugh Lofting wrote stories to amuse his son while they were on a ship traveling across the Atlantic. Poet and novelist Cecil Roberts, also aboard the ship, asked to read the stories, then convinced Lofting to submit them to his publishers. The stories developed into the Dr. Dolittle series. Roberts and Lofting never met again.

Maurice Sendak based one of the "wild things" in *Where the Wild Things Are* (1964 Caldecott Medal) on a relative who scared him as a child by saying, "I could eat you up." The other wild things were also based on Sendak's relatives.

Hardie Gramatky, creator of *Little Toot*, worked as an animator for Walt Disney Studios.

February 16

Katherine Paterson found writing about Leslie's death in *Bridge to Terabithia* (1978 Newbery Medal) difficult, but she enjoyed the revision process.

Author and illustrator William Lipkind and Nicolas Mordvinoff based *The Two Reds* (1951 Caldecott Honor Book) on their own Greenwich Village neighborhood.

Until the early 1960s, the Caldecott Medal was officially known as the "Randolph J. Caldecott Medal." Caldecott had no middle initial and no one knows how the "J." appeared.

Almost all of Judith Viorst's books for children, including *Alexander and the Terrible, Horrible, No Good, Very Bad Day* and *The Tenth Good Thing About Barney*, are based on the experiences of her own children.

February 17

 BORN ON THIS DAY:
    Robert Newton Peck, 1928
    Virginia Sorensen, 1923

The warm feelings running through *Miracles on Maple Hill* (1957 Newbery Medal) are largely based on Virginia Sorensen's own life.

Chris Van Allsburg helped write the screen story for his picture book *Jumanji* (1982 Caldecott Medal), but Tod Strasser wrote the novelization of the motion picture.

Robert Newton Peck, author of the Soup and Trig books, said *The Adventures of Tom Sawyer* strongly influenced him.

February 18

When Ellen Raskin submitted the manuscript that became the book *Figgs and Phantoms*, she said it wouldn't win the Newbery Award, but was sure to be an Honor Book—and in 1975 it was.

When *The Egg Tree* (1951 Caldecott Medal) was published, author/illustrator Katherine Milhous made fifteen egg trees with forty eggs each to send to various book stores and libraries.

Hans Christian Andersen's mother was uneducated, but she strongly encouraged her son's writing.

February 19

 BORN ON THIS DAY:
    Louis Slobodkin, 1903

Russell Freedman became interested in Eleanor Roosevelt while he worked on a biography of Franklin Roosevelt. Freedman's book *Eleanor Roosevelt* became a Newbery Honor Book in 1994.

Illustrator Louis Slobodkin and author James Thurber didn't discuss *Many Moons* (1944 Caldecott Medal) at all during the creative process.

"The Murders in the Rue Morgue" by Edgar Allan Poe is credited with being the first published detective story. The story appeared in an 1841 issue of *Graham's Magazine*.

February 20

Will James (*Smoky the Cowhorse*, 1927 Newbery Medal) served a prison sentence for cattle rustling.

Virginia Lee Burton (*The Little House*, 1943 Caldecott Medal) usually pinned sketched illustrations on the walls of her studio before writing the text for her books.

Marc Brown, creator of the Arthur books, frequently travels around the country speaking, but he says he rarely takes Arthur along because Arthur has to go to school.

February 21

During his acceptance speech, Joseph Krumgold said he and the title character in *Onion John* (1960 Newbery Medal) have something in common: a substantial gift overwhelmed each of them.

The father of Dr. Seuss (*If I Ran the Zoo*, 1951 Caldecott Honor Book) managed a zoo in Springfield, Massachusetts.

One of his elementary school teachers let Bruce Degen, illustrator of the Magic School Bus series, sit in the back of the room and paint. The teacher even let him take his spelling tests orally.

February 22

Illustrator Wesley Dennis was asked to alter his illustration of the Newgate Jail in *King of the Wind* (1949 Newbery Medal) because it looked too nice, "like a library." Dennis cheerfully revised the illustrations that he previously had been afraid to make too scary.

Author Arthur Yorinks used his profits from *Hey, Al!* (1987 Caldecott Medal) to buy property in rural Nova Scotia. Many birds inhabit the area.

J. M. Barrie sent the manuscript for *Peter Pan* to his publisher in an untidy brown-paper parcel without even a cover letter saying the work was for publication.

February 23

The father of Laura Adams Armer (*Waterless Mountain*, 1932 Newbery Medal) walked across the country behind an ox-team to settle in California in 1859.

Nicolas Sidjakov said his Russian background, as well as his four-year-old son, helped him illustrate *Babushka and the Three Kings* (1961 Caldecott Medal).

S. E. Hinton received a "D" in creative writing while she worked on the manuscript for *The Outsiders*.

February 24

 BORN ON THIS DAY:
Wilhelm Grimm, 1781

Jean Lee Latham (*Carry On, Mr. Bowditch*, 1956 Newbery Medal) started making up stories to tell her brother so he'd help her with the dishes.

Editor Walter Lorraine suggested David Macaulay write *Cathedral* (1974 Caldecott Honor Book) after seeing an illustration that Macaulay did of a boy locked in a cathedral.

Wilhelm Grimm did most of the writing and storytelling and his brother Jacob did most of the researching for their work collecting German folk and fairy tales.

February 25

 BORN ON THIS DAY:
Cynthia Voigt, 1942

Cynthia Voigt (*Dicey's Song*, 1983 Newbery Medal) calls the job of writer "one of the world's strangest occupations, full of contradictions, intensely interesting."

Marie Hall Ets (*Nine Days to Christmas*, 1960 Caldecott Medal) found drawing in Mexico City difficult because too many people gathered around her and asked questions.

George Orwell has two books on the Modern Library Board's list of 100 best novels published in the English language since 1900: *1984* is listed as number thirteen and *Animal Farm* is number thirty-one.

February 26

Hendrik Van Loon became an American citizen the same year *The Story of Mankind* (1922 Newbery Medal) was published.

Margot Zemach's (*Duffy and the Devil*, 1974 Caldecott Medal) stepfather frequently took her to art museums and galleries. He treated her as an adult during conversations about art, and he genuinely valued her opinions.

One of Nathaniel Hawthorne's ancestors was a judge in the Salem witch trials. That ancestor became the basis for a character in *The House of the Seven Gables*.

February 27

 BORN ON THIS DAY:

Henry Wadsworth Longfellow, 1807
Uri Shulevitz, 1935

The students at TASIS school in England sometimes call their headmaster, Lyle D. Rigg, "Mr. Creech" because he's married to Sharon Creech (*Walk Two Moons*, 1995 Newbery Medal).

As a baby, Uri Shulevitz (*The Fool of the World and the Flying Ship*, 1969 Caldecott Medal) scribbled on walls. By age three, he was drawing pictures. At age twelve, he won a drawing competition.

Henry Wadsworth Longfellow was the first person in America to earn a living solely by writing poetry.

February 28

 BORN ON THIS DAY:
John Tenniel, 1820

Since childhood, Elizabeth Foreman Lewis (*Young Fu of the Upper Yangtze*, 1933 Newbery Medal) lived by the motto "If worth doing at all, it is worth doing well."

As a child, Emily Arnold McCully (*Mirette on the High Wire*, 1993 Caldecott Medal) drew "two-minute" portraits during fair time. She charged twenty-five cents for each drawing.

The publication of *Alice's Adventures in Wonderland* was delayed by a year because John Tenniel didn't complete his illustrations on time, partially because Lewis Carroll requested so many changes.

February 29

Tales from Silver Lands (1925) and *Shen of the Sea* (1926) are the only books of short stories to win the top Newbery Award.

About one-fourth of all Caldecott Award-winning books (Caldecott Medal and Honor Books) have fewer than 500 words. More than half have fewer than 1,200 words. Only thirteen have more than 5,000 words.

More books about William Shakespeare have been published than about any other author.

March 1

A Visit to William Blake's Inn (1982) with rhyming text, *Joyful Noise* (1989) written with the intent to be read by two people at the same time, and *Out of the Dust* (1998) written in free verse are the only top Newbery winners written in poetry.

Chinese decorations dominated the room at the 1939 Newbery/Caldecott Awards ceremony. Frederic Melcher, who originally sponsored the idea of the Newbery and Caldecott Awards, dressed as an Oriental sage to commemorate the Caldecott winner, *Mei Li.*

Lewis Carroll stuttered.

March 2

 BORN ON THIS DAY:
Leo Dillon, 1933
Theodor Seuss Geisel (Dr. Seuss), 1904

When Katherine Paterson finished Tolkien's *The Return of the King* at the beach one day, she decided to use the name Galadriel in a book. Gilly in *The Great Gilly Hopkins* (1979 Newbery Honor Book) is a nickname for Galadriel.

While Leo Dillon (*Why Mosquitoes Buzz in People's Ears*, 1976 Caldecott Medal; *Ashanti to Zulu*, 1977 Caldecott Medal) was in art school, his only real competition was a young woman named Diane, who eventually became his collaborator and wife.

Theodore Geisel's parents gave him his mother's maiden name for a middle name. Geisel grew up to use that middle name—Seuss (along with "Dr.")—as a pen name on most of his books, including three

Caldecott Honor Books. For another pen name, he used his last name spelled backward: Theo Le Sieg.

March 3

 BORN ON THIS DAY:
Suse MacDonald, 1940
Patricia MacLachlan, 1938

The parents of Patricia MacLachlan (*Sarah, Plain and Tall*, 1986 Newbery Medal) instilled in their daughter the love of books. They read, reread, discussed, and acted out parts of books.

Suse MacDonald took her portfolio and went on forty-seven interviews with publishers and art directors before she received a contract for *Alphabatics* (1987 Caldecott Honor Book).

Robert Louis Stevenson dined with cannibal chiefs when he visited the South Seas.

March 4

 BORN ON THIS DAY:
Meindert DeJong, 1906
Dav Pilkey, 1966
Peggy Rathmann, 1953

Meindert DeJong spent four years writing *The Wheel on the School* (1955 Newbery Medal).

Dav Pilkey (*The Paperboy*, 1997 Caldecott Honor Book) hated school. He often played practical jokes that got him into trouble. When the teacher forced Pilkey to sit in the hall for being bad, he took the opportunity to draw.

The dog in *Officer Buckle and Gloria* (1996 Caldecott Medal) is based on a dog named Skipper that author/illustrator Peggy Rathmann once owned. Skipper got into trouble, but only when no one was looking.

The complete manuscript for *Adventures of Huckleberry Finn* contains 1,361 pages.

March 5

Illustrator Garth Williams traveled to all but one of the locations Laura Ingalls Wilder mentioned in her Little House books, five of which are Newbery Honor Books.

James Thurber, author of *Many Moons* (1944 Caldecott Medal), said, "With sixty staring me in the face, I have developed inflammation of the sentence structure and a definite hardening of the paragraphs."

Christopher Robin, A. A. Milne's son, named his stuffed bear Winnie-the-Pooh after an American Black Bear at the London Zoo named Winnie and a swan named Pooh.

March 6

Bette Greene (*Philip Hall Likes Me. I Reckon Maybe.*, 1975 Newbery Honor Book) credits her third-grade teacher with giving her the confidence to pursue her dream of writing.

Robert McCloskey's original idea for *Make Way for Ducklings* (1942 Caldecott Medal) was to use pigeons as the main characters, but he found pigeons too difficult to draw.

Pinocchio creator Carlo Collodi confessed to being "the most irresponsible, the most disobedient, and most impudent boy in the whole school."

March 7

The day Robert Lawson learned his editor liked the manuscript of *Rabbit Hill* (1945 Newbery Medal), he saw a rabbit, even though rabbits were scarce that year. He heard about winning the Newbery Medal the day after he saw a "Little Georgie" staring at him through a window.

Ed Emberley features some sort of parade in most of his books. A parade of people takes part in firing the cannon in *Drummer Hoff* (1968 Caldecott Medal). A parade of animals can be seen in *One Wide River to Cross* (1967 Caldecott Honor Book).

At one point in his career, Dr. Seuss spent so much time writing simple verse that even his letters came out in verse.

March 8

 BORN ON THIS DAY:
    Kenneth Grahame, 1859
    Harold Keith, 1903

In the process of researching *Rifles for Watie* (1958 Newbery Medal), Harold Keith interviewed 22 Civil War veterans. All were nearly 100 years old.

As a child, Lynd Ward's (*The Biggest Bear*, 1953 Caldecott Medal) favorite things to draw were the faces of bandits. The three main parts of the drawings were the Stetson hats, a narrow strip of the face around the eyes, and a red bandanna covering the lower part of the face.

The early versions of Kenneth Grahame's *The Wind and the Willows* also had a giraffe character.

March 9

After *Amos Fortune, Free Man* won the Newbery Medal in 1951, author Elizabeth Yates was asked to sign 3,000 copies of the book. During the three days that she spent signing the books, Yates realized she could have written an entire story for the same number of words.

David Wiesner (*Tuesday*, 1992 Caldecott Medal) seriously started working on "the frog book" while on an airplane. He worked out the whole story in an hour. He picked the day Tuesday for the "ooze" sound.

National Velvet author Enid Bagnold warned her father she intended to run away from the school she was attending—and she did, at the age of seventeen.

March 10

Many people were disappointed that Beverly Cleary's *Dear Mr. Henshaw* (1984 Newbery Medal) wasn't as humorous as her Ramona books, but others thought the book was the best writing Cleary had ever done.

The husband and wife team of Diane Dillon and Leo Dillon (*Why Mosquitoes Buzz in People's Ears*, 1976 Caldecott Medal; *Ashanti to Zulu*, 1977 Caldecott Medal) were born eleven days apart, but into different cultures: Diane is European American and Leo is African American.

Peter Pan began as a minor character in J. M. Barrie's *The Little White Bird*, published in 1902. The story of Peter Pan then became a play first performed in 1904. Finally the book, *Peter Pan and Wendy*, was published in 1911.

March 11

 BORN ON THIS DAY:
Wanda Gág, 1893
Ezra Jack Keats, 1916

After *Millions of Cats* (1929 Newbery Honor Book) was published, author/illustrator Wanda Gág's hometown newspaper in Minnesota featured a headline reading, "NEW ULM'S CINDERELLA FINDS ART'S GOLDEN SLIPPER IN NEW YORK."

Two years after World War II ended, Ezra Jack Keats (*The Snowy Day*, 1963 Caldecott Medal) changed his name from Jacob Ezra Katz to avoid anti-Semitic prejudices.

Mary Shelley's *Frankenstein* was first published on March 11, 1818.

March 12

 BORN ON THIS DAY:
Virginia Hamilton, 1936

Virginia Hamilton (*M. C. Higgins, the Great*, 1975 Newbery Medal) was the first African American writer to receive the Newbery Medal. The next African American to win the top Newbery Medal was Christopher Paul Curtis in 2000.

Margaret Wise Brown, author of *The Little Island* (1947 Caldecott Medal), under the pseudonym Golden MacDonald, is credited with being the first author to be recognized for excellent quality of writing in picture books without also being an illustrator.

At the time of *Robinson Crusoe* author Daniel Defoe's death, he was hiding from creditors.

March 13

 BORN ON THIS DAY:
Diane Dillon, 1933
Ellen Raskin, 1923

As a child, the three jobs Ellen Raskin (*The Westing Game*, 1979 Newbery Medal) wanted were musician (she practiced several hours a day until the finance company took the piano), writer (she filled many notebooks with writing), and artist. She later combined her talents by writing music and adding illustrations.

Diane Dillon (*Why Mosquitoes Buzz in People's Ears*, 1976 Caldecott Medal; and *Ashanti to Zulu*, 1977 Caldecott Medal) had to work up her courage to walk over to a fellow student named Leo and compliment him on his work. She and Leo eventually married and became collaborators.

Shel Silverstein's *A Light in the Attic* remained on the *New York Times* Bestseller List for 182 weeks.

March 14

 BORN ON THIS DAY:
Marguerite de Angeli, 1889

Marguerite de Angeli based the main character in *The Door in the Wall* (1950 Newbery Medal) on a disabled friend who led a happy and helpful life.

Nicolas Mordvinoff was so disappointed in the first proofs for *Finders Keepers* (1952 Caldecott Medal) that he started the illustrations over from scratch.

Hans Christian Andersen tried to become an actor and singer before settling into writing.

March 15

Hugh Lofting always knew which of the fan letters he received were school assignments and which were genuine fan letters for the Dr. Dolittle series, which includes *The Voyages of Dr. Dolittle* (1923 Newbery Medal).

Trina Schart Hyman's (*Saint George and the Dragon*, 1985 Caldecott Medal) daughter, Katrin, said she likes her mother's work the way other people like their mother's cooking: it's familiar.

John Newbery, the London publisher of the mid-1700s for whom the award is named, is credited with being the first person to publish books solely for children's pleasure.

Ann M. Martin, creator of the Baby-Sitters Club books, had nightmares as a child.

March 16

 BORN ON THIS DAY:
Sid Fleischman, 1920
Eric Kelly, 1884

Sid Fleischman was in the shower at the time of the phone call telling him he won the 1987 Newbery Medal for *The Whipping Boy*.

Eric Kelly wrote *The Trumpeter of Krakow* (1929 Newbery Medal) while he was teaching at the University of Krakow.

At age six, Maurice Sendak (*Where the Wild Things Are*, 1964 Caldecott Medal) completed his first full-color drawing. The drawing depicted an interest Sendak still has: Mickey Mouse, who was created the same year Sendak was born.

Charles Dickens based the character of Mr. Micawber in *David Copperfield* on his father.

March 17

 BORN ON THIS DAY:
Kate Greenaway, 1846

Lynd Ward's illustrations of animals in *The Cat Who Went to Heaven* (1931 Newbery Medal) are each as the artist in the legend painted them.

Eve Bunting (*Smoky Night*, 1995 Caldecott Medal) spent the first thirty years of her life in Ireland.

Randolph Caldecott squelched rumors of a romance between him and Kate Greenaway. He said, "She is, as you ask me, nearly thirty—maybe more—and not beautiful." Greenaway was thirty-five years old at the time, five days older than Caldecott.

March 18

A 1960 *Publishers Weekly* poll showed that *Charlotte's Web* (1953 Newbery Honor Book) is considered the best children's book written between 1930 and 1960.

Natalie Babbitt, author of *Kneeknock Rise* (1971 Newbery Honor Book) was distantly related to Zane Grey, a popular author of western novels.

Because Evaline Ness (*Sam, Bangs and Moonshine*, 1967 Caldecott Medal) had many drawings of boats in her portfolio, Sam became the daughter of a fisherman. She added Bangs to the story because her own cat sat on her artwork. She added the kangaroo after seeing a newspaper article about one.

March 19

One of Armstrong Sperry's (*Call It Courage*, 1941 Newbery Medal) earliest memories was hearing his great grandfather tell of his adventures with pirates, whales, and exotic islands when he was a ship captain.

Allen Say (*Grandfather's Journey*, 1994 Caldecott Medal) almost gave up illustrating to be a professional photographer before doing *The Boy of the Three-Year Nap* (1989 Caldecott Honor Book).

Little Women is on the list of the 100 most influential books ever published.

March 20

 BORN ON THIS DAY:
Lois Lowry, 1937
Louis Sachar, 1954

Lois Lowry (*Number the Stars*, 1990 Newbery Medal; *The Giver*, 1994 Newbery Medal) once got a fortune cookie message saying, "You will become rich and famous in a far-out profession." Lowry said she's rich, although not necessarily monetarily, as a result of her experiences as an author, but doesn't consider writing a far-out profession.

After Louis Sachar (*Holes*, 1999 Newbery Medal) and several of his friends took the bar exam, they stayed up all night to see if they passed. Sachar wasn't as excited as his friends when he learned he had passed because he wanted to be a writer instead.

A stranger who Paul Zelinsky saw in a Chinese restaurant agreed to pose as the miller's daughter in *Rumplestiltskin* (1987 Caldecott Honor Book).

Uncle Tom's Cabin by Harriet Beecher Stowe was first published March 20, 1852. At least thirty books defending slavery were published soon after Stowe's book against slavery appeared.

March 21

 BORN ON THIS DAY:
David Wisniewski, 1953

Charles Boardman Hawes (*The Dark Frigate*, 1924 Newbery Medal) often took long walks but could rarely persuade anyone to accompany him because some of the walks were twenty to thirty miles long.

When David Wisniewski (*Golem*, 1997 Caldecott Medal) first started drawing, he drew only figures in action without bothering to add clothes or faces. He later started copying pictures from comic books.

Edgar Allan Poe was expelled from West Point in 1831 for wearing the required "white belt and gloves"—but that's *all* he was wearing at the time.

March 22

 BORN ON THIS DAY:
Randolph Caldecott, 1846

The first wife of Hendrik Van Loon (*The Story of Mankind*, 1922 Newbery Medal) was a descendant of Nathaniel Bowditch, subject of *Carry On, Mr. Bowditch* (1956 Newbery Medal).

While doing research for *Abraham Lincoln* (1940 Caldecott Medal), Edgar and Ingri d'Aulaire traveled in a $25.00 car they nicknamed "Maybe" because they never knew if it would start.

Randolph Caldecott is best known for his sixteen picture books, but he also illustrated books and magazines for adults, designed wallpaper, sculpted, and produced many fine art paintings.

In 1976, *Publishers Weekly* polled teachers, librarians, authors, and publishers on the best children's books written in America. *The Wizard of Oz* was eighth on the list.

March 23

In his research for *Lincoln: A Photobiography* (1988 Newbery Medal), Russell Freedman had the opportunity to see many original Civil War and Lincoln documents and letters.

Wanda Gág rewrote and illustrated *Snow White and the Seven Dwarfs* (1939 Caldecott Honor Book) at the request of editor Anne Carroll Moore, who wanted to counter the Walt Disney version.

When Alice Liddell and her sisters were learning the game of chess, Lewis Carroll told them impromptu stories about the chess pieces. The stories grew into *Through the Looking Glass*.

March 24

While in high school, Paul Fleischman (*Joyful Noise*, 1989 Newbery Medal) wanted to write music.

John Schoenherr and Jane Yolen, illustrator and author of *Owl Moon*, met for the first time after the book won the 1988 Caldecott Medal. They went owling.

Nearly thirty publishers rejected *And to Think That I Saw It on Mulberry Street*, Dr. Seuss's first book.

March 25

The idea of writing about a pig's life being saved came to E. B. White while he was carrying a pail of slops to his pig. He added

Charlotte to the manuscript of *Charlotte's Web* (1953 Newbery Honor Book) after he noticed a large spider in the backhouse.

Karen Ackerman said illustrator Stephen Gammell's illustrations of Grandpa in *Song and Dance Man* (1989 Caldecott Medal) look a little like her father, for whom she wrote the book.

Sculptor René Paul Chambellan designed the Newbery and Caldecott Medals.

March 26

 BORN ON THIS DAY:
Robert Frost, 1874

Caddie Woodhouse was a storyteller, not a writer, so her granddaughter Carol Ryrie Brink wrote the stories which became *Caddie Woodlawn* (1936 Newbery Medal).

The idea for *Shadow* (1983 Caldecott Medal) came from a book that Marcia Brown read while she was a storyteller for the New York Public Library.

To avoid rising at dawn, Robert Frost milked his cows at 10:00 A.M.

March 27

After Laura Adams Armer won the 1932 Newbery Medal for *Waterless Mountain*, Hendrik Van Loon (*The Story of Mankind*, 1922 Newbery Medal) sent her flowers and a note thanking her for not having written her book ten years earlier.

Maurice Sendak remembers an advertisement for the Sunshine Bakers with a slogan "We Bake While You Sleep!" Sendak felt cheated since he had to go to bed while they got to have fun baking. He put those feelings into the book *In the Night Kitchen* (1971 Caldecott Honor Book).

Bernard Waber, creator of *Lyle, Lyle, Crocodile*, spent a lot of time reading picture books to himself when he took his children to the library. The children wondered why their father didn't read "grown-up" books.

March 28

The Matchlock Gun (1942 Newbery Medal) was first published in *The Saturday Evening Post* as a story for adults titled "The Spanish Gun."

Jean Craighead George (*Julie of the Wolves*, 1973 Newbery Medal) learned much about the Eskimo ways from an Eskimo woman named Julia Edwardson.

Barbara Cooney's (*Chanticleer and the Fox*, 1959 Caldecott Medal, and *Ox-Cart Man*, 1980 Caldecott Medal) mother, a painter, allowed her daughter to "mess with" her paints and brushes as much as she wanted—as long as she cleaned the brushes when she was through.

March 29

Eleanor Estes based all the characters in *Ginger Pye* (1952 Newbery Medal) on real people. Mr. Pye is a combination of Estes's husband and the father of a childhood friend; Mrs. Pye is a combination of Estes's mother, sister, self, and her imagination; Rachel and Jerry are all the children she's ever known; and Uncle Bennie is all "little uncles."

For *Rapunzel* (1998 Caldecott Medal), Paul Zelinsky purchased many art books about the Renaissance period and frequently visited the Metropolitan Museum to research art for his illustrations.

Mark Twain wanted *Adventures of Huckleberry Finn* to be about the same size as *The Adventures of Tom Sawyer* so that the books could be sold as a set.

March 30

 BORN ON THIS DAY:
Anna Sewell, 1820

Katherine Paterson thought she had made up the name Terabithia for her book *Bridge to Terabithia* (1978 Newbery Medal), but while re-reading C. S. Lewis's *The Voyage of the Dawn Treader*, she discovered an island called Terabinthia.

In *Nine Days to Christmas* (1960 Caldecott Medal), Aurora Labastida and Marie Hall Ets based their characters' personalities and appearances on actual people—except for Cici who, in real life, was too big and too blonde for a book featuring Mexican characters.

The Royal Society of the Prevention of Cruelty to Animals and the American Society for the Prevention of Cruelty to Animals adopted and distributed copies of Anna Sewell's *Black Beauty*.

March 31

 BORN ON THIS DAY:
Beni Montresor, 1926

The only money Maia Wojciechowska (*Shadow of a Bull*, 1965 Newbery Medal) had when she arrived in New York was a dime. She threw that dime into the river from the Brooklyn Bridge.

The Italian government knighted Beni Montresor (*May I Bring a Friend?*, 1965 Caldecott Medal) for his contributions to the arts.

Moby Dick was a real whale that probably first fought in 1819, the year Herman Melville was born. The whale, actually named Mocha Dick, was still terrorizing whalers in 1850 while Melville was working on the book. Mocha Dick, blind in one eye and nearly dead of old age, is said to have been killed by a Swedish whaler in 1859.

April 1

Originally the Newbery and Caldecott winners were supposed to be kept secret until the awards ceremony. In 1949, since the secret was rarely kept anyway, the rules were changed to announce the winners as soon as they were known.

When David Diaz's wife, Cecelia, once heard cheering and applause on the answering machine, she thought they'd won the Publishers Clearing House Sweepstakes. Instead, she learned *Smoky Night* had won the 1995 Caldecott Medal.

Robert Louis Stevenson was known as a practical joker and prankster.

April 2

 BORN ON THIS DAY:
Hans Christian Andersen, 1805

Mildred Taylor's (*Roll of Thunder, Hear My Cry*, 1977 Newbery Medal) first book about the Logans, *Song of the Trees*, was inspired by a real child. At one point while writing that book, Taylor lost her temper because she couldn't find the words to portray the strong feelings involved.

So far, Robert Lawson is the only person to win both a top Newbery prize (*Rabbit Hill*, 1945 Newbery Medal) and a top Caldecott prize (*They Were Strong and Good*, 1941 Caldecott Medal).

Organizers chose Hans Christian Andersen's birthday on which to celebrate International Children's Book Day.

April 3

 BORN ON THIS DAY:
Washington Irving, 1783

Betsy Byars said only her two dogs and two cats were around at the time she learned she had won the 1971 Newbery Medal for *The Summer of the Swans*. She said they looked pleased.

Because children thoroughly enjoyed the stories Jon Scieszka read to them during speaking engagements, he compiled these stories into the book *The Stinky Cheese Man and Other Fairly Stupid Tales* (1993 Caldecott Honor Book).

Some of Washington Irving's pseudonyms include Diedrich Knickerbocker, Jonathan Oldstyle, and Geoffrey Crayon.

April 4

Elizabeth George Speare (*The Witch of Blackbird Pond*, 1959 Newbery Medal, and *The Bronze Bow*, 1962 Newbery Medal) was once a part of a writing group called The Quill Drivers.

Virginia Lee Burton put her son Michael in charge of making sure people and vehicles weren't missing any parts in her illustrations for *The Little House* (1943 Caldecott Medal).

Dr. Seuss wrote *The Cat in the Hat* partially in the hope that children would be encouraged to start reading.

April 5

 BORN ON THIS DAY:
Richard Peck, 1934

Richard Peck (*A Long Way from Chicago*, 1999 Newbery Honor Book) was thirty-seven years old before he tried to write fiction.

Susan Jeffers's first version of *The Three Jovial Huntsmen* wasn't good enough to publish, but her revision made the book a 1974 Caldecott Honor Book.

Jack London's *The Call of the Wild* is eighty-eighth on the list of the Modern Library Board's 100 best novels published in the English language since 1900.

April 6

Meindert DeJong was reading reviews when a single line caught his eye. He immediately sat down and roughed out the whole book of *Shadrach* (1954 Newbery Honor Book) in one night. He was never again able to find the line that inspired him no matter how many times he went over the reviews.

Barbara Emberley had a degree in fashion design, but she still married Ed, her future collaborator on *Drummer Hoff* (1968 Caldecott Medal), in spite of the fact that he was often unshaven and wore jeans, a flannel shirt, and moccasins covered with encrusted paint.

Rudyard Kipling wrote part of *Just So Stories* in Vermont, part in Scotland, and the story "The Elephant's Child" in South Africa.

April 7

Sharon Creech received moccasins for her twelfth birthday during a trip from Ohio to Idaho. Many of her experiences are similar to Salmanaca's experiences in *Walk Two Moons* (1995 Newbery Medal).

Ingri d'Aulaire (*Abraham Lincoln*, 1940 Caldecott Medal) made a deal with her father: she agreed to have a less costly wedding, and he agreed to give her the amount saved so that she could study art in Paris.

After many publishers rejected Beatrix Potter's *Peter Rabbit*, she paid to have 450 copies printed, but she did the illustrations in black and white to save money. Frederick Warne & Company later published the book with color illustrations.

April 8

 BORN ON THIS DAY:
Trina Schart Hyman, 1939

Marcia Sewell illustrated the jacket of *Sarah, Plain and Tall* (1986 Newbery Medal) without realizing that she pictured Anna as looking very much like author Patricia MacLachlan did as a child.

Trina Schart Hyman (*Saint George and the Dragon*, 1985 Caldecott Medal) wrote and illustrated her first book when she was only four years old.

Uncle Tom's Cabin was the first novel to sell a million copies.

April 9

 BORN ON THIS DAY:
Joseph Krumgold, 1908

Joseph Krumgold (*And Now Miguel*, 1954 Newbery Medal and *Onion John*, 1960 Newbery Medal) was the first person to win the

Newbery Medal twice, a major achievement, particularly because he wrote a total of only four children's books.

Miska Petersham (*The Rooster Crows*, 1946 Caldecott Medal) once donated his last shilling to help the victims of the *Titanic* disaster.

Charles Dickens had a cat named Williamina who continually moved her kittens from the kitchen to his study, no matter how many times he moved them back. He finally gave up and learned to work while Williamina and her kittens played around him.

April 10

 BORN ON THIS DAY:
Clare Turlay Newberry, 1903

While studying in Krakow, Eric P. Kelly spent part of every day at the church that he wrote about in *The Trumpeter of Krakow* (1929 Newbery Medal).

The first thing Clare Turlay Newberry remembers drawing is a cat. She was two years old at the time. Cats play prominent roles in each of her four Caldecott Honor books.

In 1976, a *Publishers Weekly* survey of the best children's books written in America indicated that Laura Ingalls Wilder's *Little House in the Big Woods* ranked sixth and *The Little House on the Prairie* ranked ninth. The Newbery Committee didn't recognize either book.

April 11

As a child, Karen Cushman (*The Midwife's Apprentice*, 1996 Newbery Medal) enjoyed the books *Caddie Woodlawn* and *Strawberry Girl* (1936 and 1946 Newbery Medals), *Blue Willow* and *Rufus M* (1941 and 1944 Newbery Honor Books), the Bobbsey Twins books,

Mad magazine, and Little Lulu and Donald Duck comic books.

David Wiesner's (*Tuesday*, 1992 Caldecott Medal) interest in frogs began when he provided the cover illustration for the March 1989 *Cricket* magazine that featured frogs.

The headmaster at George Orwell's prep school beat him for bed-wetting.

April 12

 BORN ON THIS DAY:
Beverly Cleary, 1916

Beverly Cleary wrote *Dear Mr. Henshaw* (1984 Newbery Medal) after several children asked her to write about a boy whose parents were divorced.

In illustrating *The Treasure* (1980 Caldecott Honor Book), Uri Shulevitz tried oils, inks, opaque watercolors, and tempera paints before settling on transparent watercolors for the illustrations.

Soon after Mark Twain began writing *Adventures of Huckleberry Finn*, he said, "I'm tearing along on a new book," but he spent eight years completing the manuscript.

April 13

 BORN ON THIS DAY:
Marguerite Henry, 1902

While working on *King of the Wind* (1949 Newbery Medal), Marguerite Henry papered the walls of her study with photos that depicted scenes she was writing.

At first Allen Say was reluctant to illustrate *The Boy of the Three-Year Nap* (1989 Caldecott

Honor Book) because Japanese folktales were so familiar to him that he didn't think they were very interesting.

S. E. Hinton's boyfriend (later husband) forced her to keep working on *That Was Then, This Is Now* by refusing to take her on a date unless she had completed two pages a day.

April 14

Will James wrote *Smoky the Cowhorse* (1927 Newbery Medal) for adults. He hadn't heard of the Newbery Medal until he won it.

In 1947, Leonard Weisgard became the only illustrator to have the top Caldecott book (*The Little Island*) and an Honor Book (*Rain Drop Splash*, written by Alvin Tresselt). The following year, *White Snow, Bright Snow*, also written by Tresselt but illustrated by Roger Duvoisin, received the Caldecott Medal.

Mercer Mayer said his childhood was largely the "American, Tom Sawyer life."

April 15

 BORN ON THIS DAY:
Jacqueline Briggs Martin, 1945

In 1979, E. B. White withdrew more than $500,000 from the reserve account he had set up with his publisher to hold most of the royalties from *Charlotte's Web* (1953 Newbery Honor Book). A large portion of the funds went to pay taxes on the earnings.

When editor Ann Rider read Jacqueline Briggs Martin's manuscript for *Snowflake Bentley* (1999 Caldecott Medal), she knew Mary Azarian would be the ideal illustrator, both because her style matched the words and because both Snowflake Bentley and

Azarian are from Vermont, while Martin lives in Iowa.

The toy store F.A.O. Schwarz was going to devote an entire window featuring *The Two Reds* (1951 Caldecott Honor Book), but decided against the display because "Reds" were considered a political enemy at the time.

In the original Swedish version, *Pippi Longstocking* is titled *Pippi Langstrump*.

April 16

 BORN ON THIS DAY:
Dorothy Lathrop, 1891

Hendrik Van Loon (*The Story of Mankind*, 1922 Newbery Medal) met and became friends with Franklin Delano Roosevelt while they both were attending Harvard. Roosevelt later invited Van Loon to the White House.

Dorothy Lathrop (*Animals of the Bible*, 1938 Caldecott Medal) wanted to be a writer but was forced into drawing for financial reasons. In addition to *Animals of the Bible*, she illustrated the 1930 Newbery Medal book *Hitty: Her First Hundred Years*.

Dr. Seuss said that he couldn't draw realistically, which is why his characters tend to look unusual.

April 17

Nancy Willard (*A Visit to William Blake's Inn*, 1982 Newbery Medal and Caldecott Honor Book) was seven years old when her first published poem appeared in a church magazine.

To get the goat to lick the boy's hand while making the film version of *Zlateh the Goat* (1967 Newbery Honor Book), the director had to sprinkle salt and bread crumbs on the boy's hand. Unfortunately, the goat tended to bite instead of lick!

Poet Langston Hughes wrote to Ezra Jack Keats to say he wished he had a grandchild to whom he could give the book *The Snowy Day* (1963 Caldecott Medal).

April 18

Eleanor Estes wore a strapless dress the night she received the 1952 Newbery Medal for *Ginger Pye*. Her editor Margaret McElderry later inadvertently called the dress "topless."

The 1955 Newbery book was *The Wheel on the School*, a story about storks building their nests on roofs in Holland. One of the 1955 Caldecott Honor Books was *Wheel on the Chimney* about storks building their nests on roofs in Hungary.

Robert D. San Souci wrote *The Talking Eggs* (1990 Caldecott Honor Book), illustrated by Jerry Pinkney. He also wrote *The Faithful Friend* (1996 Caldecott Honor Book), which was illustrated by Brian Pinkney, the son of Jerry Pinkney.

April 19

 BORN ON THIS DAY:
Eric Knight, 1897
Jean Lee Latham, 1902

Jean Lee Latham (*Carry On, Mr. Bowditch*, 1956 Newbery Medal) became interested in Nathaniel Bowditch after picking up his book and realizing she couldn't understand the text.

Leo Dillon and Diane Dillon put a little red bird in every scene of *Why Mosquitoes Buzz in People's Ears* (1976 Caldecott Medal). The bird wasn't a part of the story but simply watched the action.

Eric Knight wrote a short story imagining what happened to his dog after she became lost in the woods while chasing a rabbit. He was persuaded to expand the story into the book *Lassie Come Home*.

April 20

Russell Freedman (*Lincoln: A Photobiography*, 1988 Newbery Medal) once sat in the back row of Ford's Theatre in Washington, D.C., and tried to imagine the scene the night Lincoln was shot.

In 1944 *Many Moons*, written by James Thurber and illustrated by Louis Slobodkin, received the Caldecott Medal. In 1990, Harcourt Brace Jovanovich published Thurber's text of *Many Moons* with illustrations by Marc Simont, who also illustrated *A Tree Is Nice* (1957 Caldecott Medal).

Translators and others have expanded, condensed, or otherwise changed the original version of *Swiss Family Robinson* so that now more than 200 versions are known to exist.

April 21

The idea for *From the Mixed-up Files of Mrs. Basil E. Frankweiler* (1968 Newbery Medal) came from a family trip during which E. L. Konigsburg's family had to "rough it" in Yellowstone National Park.

David Macaulay spent seven years creating *Black and White* (1991 Caldecott Medal).

Robert Louis Stevenson drew an imaginary map to amuse his stepson. Stevenson wrote *Treasure Island* to explain the map.

April 22

 BORN ON THIS DAY:
Paula Fox, 1923

Because Paula Fox (*The Slave Dancer*, 1974 Newbery Medal) is of European descent, she has been criticized for writing about slavery.

In his acceptance speech for *Jumanji* (1982 Caldecott Medal), Chris Van Allsburg thanked artists Vermeer and Degas for their techniques, *M*A*S*H* character Max Klinger for the way he told a story, Fellini for the way his films look, and Harold for his purple crayon.

Edgar Allan Poe often wrote poems with his Siamese cat sitting on his shoulder.

April 23

 BORN ON THIS DAY:
William Shakespeare, 1564

Elizabeth Yates was making a birthday cake for a young friend when a special delivery letter arrived with the news that *Amos Fortune, Free Man* had won the 1951 Newbery Medal.

When Katherine Milhous (*The Egg Tree*, 1951 Caldecott Medal) learned that the original egg trees were a sign of fertility, she didn't know if a publisher would risk releasing a book about egg trees. She nearly gave up on the project but persisted until Scribner published the book.

William Shakespeare died on his 52nd birthday.

April 24

 BORN ON THIS DAY:
Daniel Defoe, 1731
Evaline Ness, 1911

Sharon Creech compared winning the 1995 Newbery Medal for *Walk Two Moons* to getting the meatball in a plate of spaghetti.

Evaline Ness's (*Sam, Bangs and Moonshine*, 1967 Caldecott Medal) marriage to Eliot Ness, who was best known for his work with the FBI, ended in divorce.

Daniel Defoe spent time in jail because of the satirical writing he did opposing intolerance.

April 25

Susan Cooper wrote *Over Sea Under Stone* after seeing an advertisement for a writing contest which called for a family adventure story. The book was the first in a series that included *The Dark Is Rising* (1974 Newbery Honor Book) and *The Grey King* (1976 Newbery Medal).

Gene Zion's (*All Falling Down*, 1952 Caldecott Honor Book) interest in art began in kindergarten when his teacher complimented him on his crayon border on a sheet of paper. Even so, he wrote *All Falling Down* and his wife, Margaret Bloy Graham, illustrated it.

Lewis Carroll was fussy about every detail in the illustrations for his books about Alice.

April 26

Katherine Paterson became a foster mother for two months. She wrote *The Great Gilly Hopkins* (1979 Newbery Honor Book) as a confession that she "treated her foster children like Kleenex"—as something to be discarded.

Robert McCloskey was walking through the Public Garden in Boston on his way to art school when he got the original idea for *Make Way for Ducklings* (1942 Caldecott Award). Four years later he saw ducks causing a traffic jam which renewed the idea.

The Poky Little Puppy, written by Janette Sebring Lowrey and illustrated by Gustaf Tenggren, was published in 1942. It is the most popular Little Golden Book.

April 27

 BORN ON THIS DAY:
Ludwig Bemelmans, 1898

Many people asked Robert C. O'Brien why he picked rats as heroes of *Mrs. Frisby and the Rats of NIMH* (1972 Newbery Medal). He replied that he couldn't remember.

Editor May Massee persuaded Ludwig Bemelmans (*Madeline's Rescue*, 1954 Caldecott Medal) to write and illustrate children's books after she saw the murals he had painted on the walls of the restaurant he owned.

Ernest Hemingway's cats refused to sleep on the bed with him if he were drunk.

April 28

 BORN ON THIS DAY:
Lois Duncan, 1934
Harper Lee, 1926

The mother of Virginia Sorensen (*Miracles on Maple Hill*, 1957 Newbery Medal) said her daughter's first sentence was "Tell me a story" and her second was "I'll tell you a story."

Gerald McDermott's film *Anansi the Spider* won the Blue Ribbon for children's films at the American Film Festival in 1970. His book version of the story was a 1973 Caldecott Honor Book.

Lois Duncan once registered for a class in children's literature under her real name, Lois Arquette. The teacher, not realizing the identity of her student, assigned a Lois Duncan book for the class to analyze. Arquette received an "A."

To Kill a Mockingbird by Harper Lee won the Pulitzer Prize for fiction in 1961.

April 29

Cynthia Rylant has almost no memory of writing *Missing May* (1993 Newbery Medal). She simply let Summer, the main character, start talking.

Paul Goble (*The Girl Who Loved Wild Horses*, 1979 Caldecott Medal) became interested in Native American culture after his mother read him stories by Grey Owl and Ernest Thompson Seton.

Twenty-six publishers rejected the first Encyclopedia Brown book.

April 30

Emily Neville owned a cat named "Cat" while she wrote *It's Like This, Cat* (1964 Newbery Medal).

Maurice Sendak once planned to illustrate a collection of nursery rhymes and started writing down his favorites. He suddenly realized they all concerned food. Sendak altered his plans and started a new project that became *In the Night Kitchen* (1971 Caldecott Honor Book).

At about age seven, Judith Viorst's first attempt at writing was an ode to her dead parents, but at the time, her parents were still alive!

May 1

Ellen Raskin based the character of Angela in *The Westing Game* (1979 Newbery Medal) mostly on herself.

Elizabeth Orton Jones borrowed actual toys to use for the illustrations in *Prayer for a Child* (1945 Caldecott Medal). A girl posed for each of the scenes in the book as well.

Uncle Remus by Joel Chandler Harris is considered one of the 100 most influential books.

May 2

Phyllis Reynolds Naylor wrote the first draft of *Shiloh* (1992 Newbery Medal) "at breakneck speed." She said the writing was "as though Marty himself were perched on the arm of my chair telling me the story in his own way."

At a party, Paul Zelinsky, using various cheeses, once built the tower from *Rapunzel* (1998 Caldecott Medal) as big as a table.

Randolph Caldecott pronounced his name "*Call*-da-cott," but the award is the "*Cal* [like in *Cali*fornia]-da-cott" Medal.

May 3

 BORN ON THIS DAY:
Mavis Jukes, 1947

Mavis Jukes (*Like Jake and Me*, 1985 Newbery Honor Book) didn't plan to be a writer while growing up because she "grew up in the '50s, when girls didn't know that girls grew up to be anything."

When David Diaz first read Eve Bunting's manuscript for *Smoky Night* (1995 Caldecott

Medal), he thought the book could help people become more tolerant and less prejudiced.

Herman Melville once spent a month with the Typee Valley cannibals in the Marquesas Islands.

May 4

 BORN ON THIS DAY:
Don Wood, 1945

Nancy Willard asked the Provensens to draw William Blake in *A Visit to William Blake's Inn* (1982 Newbery Medal and Caldecott Honor Book) to resemble the actual man.

As a child, Don Wood (*King Bidgood's in the Bathtub*, 1986 Caldecott Honor Book) drew on sheets of tan laundry paper. That way, he could draw a whole story on one sheet instead of needing several pages.

Mark Twain gave his cats names like Blatherstike and Zoraster to teach his children how to pronounce difficult words.

May 5

E. B. White's notes on *Charlotte's Web* (1953 Newbery Honor Book) include a detailed description of how to care for pigs, facts about spiders, and possibilities of what words Charlotte would weave into her web.

Leo Dillon and Diane Dillon researched *Ashanti to Zulu* (1977 Caldecott Medal) extensively. They spent many hours in bookstores searching for back issues of *National Geographic* magazines and spoke to experts in African culture at the United Nations and Yale University.

Louise Fatio got the idea for *The Happy Lion* from an incident in which a lion escaped from a circus near her home.

May 6

 BORN ON THIS DAY:
Judy Delton, 1931

Dr. Dolittle first appeared in letters written by Hugh Lofting (*The Voyages of Dr. Dolittle*, 1923 Newbery Medal) to his children. Lofting's son, Collin, was nicknamed Dr. Dolittle.

Arthur Yorinks and Richard Egielski, author and illustrator of *Hey, Al!* (1987 Caldecott Medal), saw each other for the first time in an elevator.

Judy Delton, author of the Pee Wee Scouts, Angel, and Kitty books, says she didn't write anything beyond "a note to the milkman" until she was 40 years old.

May 7

 BORN ON THIS DAY:
Nonny Hogrogian, 1932
Randall Jarrell, 1914

Randall Jarrell thought *The Animal Family* (1966 Newbery Honor Book) wouldn't be suitable for illustration, except maybe with photographs. Illustrator Maurice Sendak agreed and "decorated" the book instead of "illustrating" it. Jarrell considers the work among Sendak's best.

Being allergic to ice cream cones never stopped Nonny Hogrogian (*Always Room for One More*, 1966 Caldecott Medal; *One Fine Day*, 1972 Caldecott Medal) from eating them anyway.

Edgar Allan Poe won a prize for his story "Ms. Found in a Bottle." The judges said their decision was made partially "by the beauty of his handwriting."

May 8

May 8 is the traditional day for the arrival of storks at Ribe, Denmark. Meindert DeJong (*The Wheel on the School*, 1955 Newbery Medal) "migrated" to the United States when he was eight years old.

Nancy Tafuri's husband gave her the idea for *Have You Seen My Duckling?* (1985 Caldecott Honor Book) when he said a story about the mallard mother and her ducklings on their property would make a great book.

Charles Dickens cat named The Master's Cat had a habit of snuffing out the candle while Dickens was trying to work.

May 9

 BORN ON THIS DAY:
J. M. Barrie, 1860
William Pène du Bois, 1916
Eleanor Estes, 1906

William Pène du Bois wrote *The Twenty-One Balloons* (1948 Newbery Medal) while serving in the army. He submitted the manuscript to a publisher on the day he became a civilian again.

Just before Eleanor Estes drew the pictures for *Ginger Pye* (1952 Newbery Medal), she had been drawing upside down so her daughter could see drawings right-side-up. Estes had to get used to drawing "straight on" again.

J. M. Barrie said that after his first book was published, he carried it around with him and frequently checked to make sure the ink hadn't faded.

May 10

Of the many times Katherine Paterson answered *"Jacob Have I Loved"* (1981 Newbery Medal) when asked the title of her new book, only one person replied, "But Esau have I hated," a continuation of the verse.

Maurice Sendak originally intended his book to be *Where the Wild Horses Are*, but he found horses too difficult to draw. He decided to change his title to *Where the Wild Things Are* (1964 Caldecott Medal) on May 10, 1963.

In 1975, the best-selling children's book of the twentieth century was *Green Eggs and Ham*, which sold about two million copies with sales still going strong.

May 11

 BORN ON THIS DAY:
Sheila Burnford, 1918
Mari Sandoz, 1901
Zilpha Keatley Snyder, 1927

The state of Nebraska celebrates the birthday of Mari Sandoz (*The Horsecatcher*, 1958 Newbery Honor Book) in honor of her work on the era of the American pioneers.

Student Zilpha Keatley Snyder taught at Berkeley. A game her daughter played inspired Snyder to write *The Egypt Game* (1968 Newbery Honor Book).

Dorothy Lathrop said she wished the audience at her acceptance speech for *Animals of the Bible* (1938 Caldecott Medal) was made up

of animals, so she could look at furry faces and know better what to say.

Sheila Burnford based the personalities of the animals in *The Incredible Journey* on her family's pets: a Siamese kitten named Simon, a bull terrier named Bill, and a Labrador retriever.

May 12

In 1936, Robert Lawson (*Rabbit Hill*, 1945 Newbery Medal) and his wife built a home they called Rabbit Hill.

Ezra Jack Keats cut patterns in gum erasers and dipped them in paint to stamp on the paper to make snowflakes for *The Snowy Day* (1963 Caldecott Medal).

Kenneth Grahame told the first *Wind in the Willows* story in honor of his son's fourth birthday on May 12, 1904.

May 13

When Walter Edmonds's editor learned *The Matchlock Gun* (1942) had won the Newbery Medal, he sent 1,000 copies of the book for Edmonds to sign. Edmonds felt sorry for the mail carrier and bought a truck to get his own cartons from the post office.

When a sixteen-year-old Ludwig Bemelmans (*Madeline's Rescue*, 1954 Caldecott Medal) came to the United States from Europe in 1914, he made sure he had two pistols and plenty of ammunition to protect himself from the American Indians he'd read about in books.

The original toys on which *Winnie-the-Pooh* was based are displayed in a glass case at the publishing offices of E. P. Dutton.

May 14

 BORN ON THIS DAY:
George Selden, 1929

George Selden's (*The Cricket in Times Square*, 1961 Newbery Honor Book) real name is George Selden Thompson, but he dropped the Thompson because another writer already had the name George Thompson.

Lois Lowry (*The Giver*, Newbery Medal) and Allen Say (*Grandfather's Journey*, Caldecott Medal) sat at the same table during the 1994 awards ceremony. They learned that they had lived in Tokyo at the same time when they were children. They may have even seen each other because Lowry lived around the corner from Say's school.

Nathaniel Hawthorne's *Twice-Told Tales* and *The Scarlet Letter* are both on the list of 100 most influential books.

May 15

 BORN ON THIS DAY:
L. Frank Baum, 1856

Elizabeth Enright (*Thimble Summer*, 1939 Newbery Medal) once wanted to be a ballet dancer, but her many hours of practice didn't get her anything but sore toes.

Byrd Baylor, author of four Caldecott Honor Books (*When Clay Sings*, 1973; *The Desert Is Theirs*, 1976; *Hawk, I'm Your Brother*, 1977; and *The Way to Start a Day*, 1979), has vivid memories of her childhood spent largely outdoors. She was even allowed to sit under a mesquite tree to study while she was attending school.

Lyman Frank Baum wrote under many names including L. Frank Baum, Frank L. Baum, Floyd Akens, and Edith Van Dyne.

May 16

 BORN ON THIS DAY:
Bruce Coville, 1950
Wesley Dennis, 1903

Wesley Dennis (illustrator of *King of the Wind*, 1949 Newbery Medal) became interested in the Godolphin Arabian after someone hired him to draw the horse for stationery letterhead. Dennis convinced Marguerite Henry to write about the horse.

A 1983 apartment fire destroyed all of David Wiesner's (*Tuesday*, 1992 Caldecott Medal) work up to that time.

Bruce Coville, author of *My Teacher Is an Alien* and other books, regrets the time he spent watching television as a child when he could have been reading instead.

May 17

 BORN ON THIS DAY:
Gary Paulsen, 1939

Gary Paulsen, author of Newbery Honor Books *Dogsong* (1986), *Hatchet* (1988), and *The Winter Room* (1990), survived a storm while he was in a fiberglass sailboat on the Pacific Ocean.

The scene on the back jacket of *Saint George and the Dragon* (1985 Caldecott Medal) is of author Margaret Hodges and her husband on their way to meet illustrator Trina Schart Hyman.

The Caldecott and Newbery Honor Books were called Runners-up until 1977 when officials decided that the term didn't give enough credit to the excellence of books that were finalists in consideration for the top awards.

May 18

 BORN ON THIS DAY:
Irene Hunt, 1907

Irene Hunt spent many years at her kitchen table "pounding the typewriter" until late at night. Her number of publication rejections grew until *Across Five Aprils*, the sole Newbery Honor Book in 1965.

After receiving the Caldecott Medal for *A Tree Is Nice* (1957), Marc Simont had so many requests for his biography, he started thinking the facts about his life sounded like they belonged to someone else.

Copies of *Robinson Crusoe* sold so quickly when first published that four additional printings were needed within four months.

May 19

During the 1920s, all top Newbery Medal authors were men, but in the 1930s, all top Newbery Medal authors were women.

While Tom Feelings was working on *Jambo Means Hello* (1975 Caldecott Honor Book), high humidity created problems with the tissue paper he used in the art.

According to Robert Newton Peck, the character of Miss Kelly, the teacher in the Soup books, is based on a real teacher and is portrayed with almost 100 percent accuracy.

May 20

Cynthia Rylant wanted to write about someone who was mesmerizing, so she developed the character of the preacher in *A Fine White Dust* (1987 Newbery Honor Book).

Although Jane Yolen based the child in *Owl Moon* (1988 Caldecott Medal) on her daughter, the book doesn't specify whether the child is a boy or girl.

Charles Dickens had small, sloppy handwriting, usually done in blue ink on blue paper.

May 21

Almost sixteen years to the day elapsed between the time Armstrong Sperry first saw the island of Bora Bora, on which he based *Call It Courage*, and the day he accepted the 1941 Newbery Medal for the book.

Peggy Rathmann's (*Officer Buckle and Gloria*, 1996 Caldecott Medal) first book, *Ruby the Copycat*, developed from her urge to steal stories from others in a writing and illustrating class.

Especially in his later books, Dr. Seuss simply wrote without being concerned about the age of his audience.

May 22

 BORN ON THIS DAY:
Arnold Lobel, 1933

Paul Fleischman (*Joyful Noise*, 1989 Newbery Medal) usually did his homework on the bus.

Editor Charlotte Zolotow suggested Arnold Lobel select fables to illustrate for a book. Lobel read fables by Aesop, but the violence in them discouraged him. When a broken ankle forced him into inactivity, he wrote his own fables. The resulting book, *Fables*, became the 1981 Caldecott Medal winner.

Ernest Hemingway owned many cats. Many of his cats' descendants still live in and around the author's house in Key West, Florida.

May 23

 BORN ON THIS DAY:

Susan Cooper, 1935

Golden MacDonald [pseudonym of Margaret Wise Brown], 1910

Scott O'Dell, 1898

After winning the 1976 Newbery Medal for *The Grey King*, Susan Cooper credited her success to the influence of two of her professors: J. R. R. Tolkien and C. S. Lewis.

Scott O'Dell was writing an informal history about California when he found an article about a young Indian girl who had spent eighteen years alone on an island. That article sparked the idea for *Island of the Blue Dolphins* (1961 Newbery Medal).

Golden MacDonald, the pen name of Margaret Wise Brown (*The Little Island*, 1947 Caldecott Medal), once owned thirty-six rabbits, two squirrels, a collie, two guinea pigs, a Belgian hare, seven fish, and a wild robin—simultaneously.

May 24

 BORN ON THIS DAY:

Elizabeth Lewis, 1892

While Elizabeth Lewis (*Young Fu of the Upper Yangtze*, 1933 Newbery Medal) lived in China, people told her how rich she was simply because she had a small collection of books.

Stephen Gammell (*Song and Dance Man*, 1989 Caldecott Medal) prefers not to conduct research if he can manage without it; instead, he draws from his imagination.

Roald Dahl was severely injured in World War II.

May 25

The film version of *Zlateh the Goat* (1967 Newbery Honor Book) won many international film awards.

Although *McElligot's Pool* was a Caldecott Honor Book in 1948, Theodor Seuss Geisel (Dr. Seuss) didn't consider it as successful as his other books because children didn't like it as well. He illustrated the book without the hard black outlines used in his other books.

When Edgar Allan Poe was too poor to afford heat, he and his wife took turns holding the family cat for warmth.

May 26

At Charles Boardman Hawes's (*The Dark Frigate*, 1924 Newbery Medal) request, his son called him "The Old Man."

The first Newbery Medal recipient, awarded in 1922, was selected by popular vote. *The Story of Mankind* was the landslide winner with 163 votes while 14 other books received a combined total of 49 votes.

William Steig (*Sylvester and the Magic Pebble*, 1970 Caldecott Medal) said that although giving an acceptance speech is difficult for a shy person, he "wouldn't mind going through that suffering again."

May 27

Martin H. Greenberg and Charles G. Waugh collected stories by Newbery Medal winners under various themes including *A Newbery Christmas* (1991), *A Newbery Halloween* (1993), and *A Newbery Zoo* (1995), all published by Delacorte.

When Ed Young (*Lon Po Po*, 1990 Caldecott Medal) once brought home a bad report card, his mother said, "Eddy, I wonder what is to become of you."

Hardie Gramatky got the idea for *Little Toot* from watching the boats on the East River go past the window of his studio in New York City.

May 28

 BORN ON THIS DAY:
Ian Fleming, 1908

In high school, Mildred Taylor (*Roll of Thunder, Hear My Cry*, 1977 Newbery Medal) was a class officer, was a member of the honor society, and worked on the school newspaper, but she wanted to be a cheerleader.

David Wisniewski (*Golem*, 1997 Caldecott Medal) uses between 800 and 1,000 blades for his knife to create the illustrations for each book.

Ian Fleming, author of *Chitty Chitty Bang Bang*, is best known for creating the character of Agent 007—James Bond.

May 29

Cornelia Meigs gave most of the credit for *Invincible Louisa* (1934 Newbery Medal) to Louisa May Alcott.

During her acceptance speech for *Once a Mouse* (1962 Caldecott Medal), Marcia Brown told a similar version of the story set in the publishing world.

The unsold stock of a limited edition of a leather-bound edition of Rudyard Kipling's poem "If" was destroyed in a World War II air raid. The surplus red leather was used to upholster chairs in the publisher's offices.

May 30

A note Karen Cushman sent with the manuscript for *The Midwife's Apprentice* (1996 Newbery Medal) read, "I don't know if this is a book or a writing exercise."

At the time Cynthia Voigt won the 1983 Newbery Medal for *Dicey's Song*, her five-year-old son called it "The Blueberry Award."

Beni Montresor (*May I Bring a Friend?* 1965 Caldecott Medal) described the Caldecott Medal as "the Nobel Prize of children's books."

May 31

 BORN ON THIS DAY:
Elizabeth Coatsworth, 1893
Walt Whitman, 1819
Jay Williams, 1914

Visiting many Buddhist temples inspired Elizabeth Coatsworth to write *The Cat Who Went to Heaven* (1931 Newbery Medal).

In 1938, Helen Dean Fish selected the text for both the top Caldecott book, *Animals of the Bible*, and the Caldecott Honor Book *Four and Twenty Blackbirds*.

Jay Williams and Raymond Abrashkin started work on *Danny Dunn and the Anti-Gravity Paint* while Abrashkin was almost completely paralyzed by illness. Abrashkin couldn't speak, so he pointed to letters. Eventually, he had to communicate by blinking his eyes.

Walt Whitman typeset and paid for the original printing of *Leaves of Grass* himself.

June 1

 BORN ON THIS DAY:
James Daugherty, 1889

James Daugherty's (*Daniel Boone*, 1940 Newbery Medal) grandfather often told him stories about Daniel Boone.

Louis Sachar (*Holes*, 1999 Newbery Medal) doesn't like hot weather.

A few hours before Nonny Hogrogian learned she had won the 1972 Caldecott Medal for *One Fine Day*, she said she thought winning another Caldecott in addition to *Always Room for One More* (1966) would be great.

Lewis Carroll considered many possible titles for his book about Alice including *Alice Among the Elves/Goblins* and *Alice's Hour/Doings/Adventures in Elf-land/Wonderland*.

June 2

Marguerite de Angeli called winning the 1950 Newbery Medal for *The Door in the Wall* "a wonderful open door."

Ed Emberly (*Drummer Hoff*, 1968 Caldecott Medal) spent two years serving in an army parade unit on Governor's Island.

While working on *1984*, George Orwell said, "Writing a book is a horrible, exhausting struggle, like a long bout of some painful illness."

June 3

Sid Fleischman was doing research for another project when he got the idea for *The Whipping Boy* (1987 Newbery Medal).

The first time Blair Lent (*The Funny Little Woman*, 1973 Caldecott Medal) became aware of the Caldecott Medal was when he saw its sticker on the cover of one of his favorite picture books: *The Little House* (1943 Caldecott Medal).

William Shakespeare's last name is spelled "Shagspere" on his marriage license and "Shakspeare" on his monument.

June 4

Libraries in at least half of the states refused to stock *The Story of Mankind* (1922 Newbery Medal) because of author Hendrik Van Loon's discussion of evolution.

Alice Provensen and Martin Provensen didn't consciously try to include the idea of "If at first you don't succeed, try, try again" in *The Glorious Flight* (1984 Caldecott Medal).

One night, Robert Louis Stevenson's wife woke him because she thought he was having a nightmare. The dream he was having became the basis for *Dr. Jekyll and Mr. Hyde*.

June 5

 BORN ON THIS DAY:
Richard Scarry, 1919

E. L. Konigsburg said winning the 1968 Newbery Medal for *From the Mixed-up Files of Mrs. Basil E. Frankweiler* gave her the courage to experiment with her writing.

Many of the illustrations for *In the Night Kitchen* (1971 Caldecott Honor Book) contain bits of information about Maurice Sendak's life. For example, a cream carton shows the two addresses where he lived as a boy, and his birthdate appears on a coconut carton.

Richard Scarry said he didn't learn much in school and didn't go to college because "no college would have me." He did attend the Boston Museum School of Fine Arts.

June 6

 BORN ON THIS DAY:
Verna Aardema, 1911
Will James, 1892
Cynthia Rylant, 1954
Peter Spier, 1927

Will James (*Smoky the Cowhorse*, 1927 Newbery Medal) fell off a bucking horse and was severely injured. While he was recuperating, he started drawing and wrote stories to accompany his drawings.

Cynthia Rylant (*Missing May*, 1993 Newbery Medal) didn't feel like a writer until after her seventh book.

Verna Aardema (*Why Mosquitoes Buzz in People's Ears*, 1976 Caldecott Medal) credited her daughter, Paula, for her writing career. Paula refused to eat unless her mother made up stories for her.

Peter Spier's father owned a complete set of Randolph Caldecott's Picture Books. At the age of three, Peter was spanked for scribbling with a red crayon on every page of one of those books. When Peter won the Caldecott Medal for *Noah's Ark* in 1978, his father gave him that set of Caldecott books.

June 7

Katherine Paterson gave Gilly in *The Great Gilly Hopkins* (1979 Newbery Honor Book) the last name Hopkins after the poet Gerard Manley Hopkins.

Librarian Aurora Labastida suggested the story for *Nine Days to Christmas* (1960 Caldecott Medal) to illustrator Marie Hall Ets. Labastida wanted a book showing that people in Mexico have modern conveniences.

Roald Dahl said he wouldn't have written children's books if he hadn't had children. He wrote all his books for his own children.

June 8

Meindert DeJong (*The Wheel on the School*, 1955 Newbery Medal) was born on a day that the sea rose higher than the dike and flooded the area. He and his mother spent several days in the attic to escape the water.

A sculpture of Mrs. Mallard and her ducklings from *Make Way for Ducklings* (1942 Caldecott Medal) now stands in Boston's Public Garden. Someone once stole one of the ducklings.

Alexandre Dumas's pet monkeys once opened the door to the aviary where Dumas kept his exotic birds. Dumas's cat Mysouff II ate the entire collection of birds.

June 9

As a child, Hugh Lofting (*The Voyages of Dr. Dolittle*, 1923 Newbery Medal) hid a variety of small animals and developed a small "natural history museum" in his mother's linen closet—until his mother discovered the secret.

George Selden called Garth Williams's illustrations in *The Cricket in Times Square* (1961 Newbery Honor Book) "inhumanly beautiful . . . inhumanly, I mean, because they're of animals."

Paul Zelinsky based several of his illustrations in *Rapunzel* (1998 Caldecott Medal) on scenes of well-known, 500-year-old paintings.

June 10

 BORN ON THIS DAY:
Maurice Sendak, 1928

Kate Seredy (*Dobry*, 1935 Newbery Medal) said her writing secret is that her stories come from "out of nowhere."

As a child, Maurice Sendak (*Where the Wild Things Are*, 1964 Caldecott Medal) thoroughly enjoyed the first book he received; he even tasted it.

Clement Hurd, illustrator of *The Runaway Bunny*, once made his living primarily by painting murals in bathrooms.

June 11

In the illustration for "Bye Baby Bunting" in *The Rooster Crows* (1946 Caldecott Medal), the mother is sitting on the wrong side of the cow (cows should be milked from their right side, not their left), and she is milking too close to the front of the cow.

Caddie Woodhouse, on whom Carol Ryrie Brink based *Caddie Woodlawn* (1936 Newbery Medal), never returned to the place where she grew up, but her vivid descriptions of the area allowed Brink to find the places in her grandmother's stories.

For a pen name, William S. Porter used the name of a guard at the Ohio penitentiary where he was serving time. The guard's name: O. Henry.

June 12

 BORN ON THIS DAY:
Johanna Spyri, 1827

Virginia Hamilton started *M. C. Higgins, the Great* (1975 Newbery Medal) and then suffered writer's block. She put the manuscript away for a few years before she finally finished the book.

Leo Dillon and Diane Dillon originally considered incorporating each letter of the alphabet into the illustrations in *Ashanti to Zulu* (1977 Caldecott Medal).

Very little of the childhood of Johanna Spyri, author of *Heidi*, is known because she was a very private person.

June 13

Laura Adams Armer wrote her first book, *Waterless Mountain* (1932 Newbery Medal), at age 57.

As a child, Ezra Jack Keats (*The Snowy Day*, 1963 Caldecott Medal) once drew all over the kitchen table. Instead of making him wash it off, his mother covered the table with a cloth to preserve the work to show to friends and neighbors.

Rudyard Kipling invented winter golf and painted the golf balls red, so he could see them in the snow.

June 14

 BORN ON THIS DAY:
Janice May Udry, 1928
Laurence Yep, 1948

Laurence Yep, author of the Newbery Honor Books *Dragonwings* (1976) and *Dragon's Gate* (1994) was eighteen when his first story was published. He received a penny a word.

Janice May Udry wrote *A Tree Is Nice* (1957 Caldecott Medal) after she saw an area where many trees had been cut down to make room for a housing development.

Louisa May Alcott used the pseudonyms Flora Fairfield and A. M. Barnard in addition to her own name when writing.

June 15

Elizabeth George Speare (*The Witch of Blackbird Pond*, 1959 Newbery Medal and *The Bronze Bow*, 1962 Newbery Medal) wrote her first novel at the age of eight. She described it as "an incredibly dull imitation of the Bobbsey Twins."

The idea for *All Falling Down* (1952 Caldecott Honor Book) began with a sketch that Margaret Bloy Graham had done of children gathering apples in an orchard.

Frederic Melcher suggested a medal be awarded for the book chosen as "the most distinguished contribution to children's literature" instead of a monetary prize because the Children's Librarians Section of the American Library Association had only $1.95 in their treasury at the time the first Newbery was presented.

June 16

At age seven, Paula Fox (*The Slave Dancer*, 1974 Newbery Medal) wrote a bloody detective story.

Edgar Parin d'Aulaire's (*Abraham Lincoln*, 1940 Caldecott Medal) grandfather from Texas enlisted in Lincoln's army at age sixteen.

Goodnight Moon, a perennial favorite of children, was not a Caldecott Medal-winning book or even an Honor Book.

June 17

E. L. Konigsburg used Mozart's *Symphony #40 in G Minor* as the model for *The View from Saturday* (1997 Newbery Medal) with a recurrent theme and melody that are separate, yet intertwined.

The number of Caldecott Honor Books selected in a year has ranged from one to five, while the number of Newbery Honor Books has ranged from one to eight.

Sherley Ann Williams's (*Working Cotton*, 1993 Caldecott Honor Book) book of verse, *The Peacock Poems*, received a Pulitzer Prize nomination.

Mark Twain wrote the first part of *Adventures of Huckleberry Finn* in black ink and the last part in purple ink. He revised in black ink, gray ink, and pencil.

June 18

 BORN ON THIS DAY:
Chris Van Allsburg, 1949

Katherine Paterson took a friend's suggestion and said, "We have to stop meeting like this" during her acceptance speech for her second Newbery Medal book, *Jacob Have I Loved* (1981).

The first book Chris Van Allsburg (*Jumanji*, 1982 Caldecott Medal, and *The Polar Express*, 1986 Caldecott Medal) checked out of the library was a biography of Babe Ruth. He read the book all the way through without stopping, not because the book was especially good, but because he was used to seeing the end of a story on TV.

Judy Blume's first books (unpublished), were rhyming stories she made up while doing the dishes.

June 19

Russell Freedman (*Lincoln: A Photobiography*, 1988 Newbery Medal) remembers reading *The Story of Mankind* (1922 Newbery Medal) on the maroon sofa in the living room of his childhood home.

Richard Peck (*A Long Way from Chicago*, 1999 Newbery Honor Book) once appeared as an imposter on the TV game show *To Tell the Truth*. Peck's answers to medical questions caused two of the four celebrity panelists to incorrectly vote for him.

An inspiration for Maurice Sendak's *Outside over There* (1982 Caldecott Honor Book) was the Charles Lindbergh baby kidnapping—except Sendak gave the book a happier ending than the Lindbergh story.

June 20

While in school, William Pène du Bois (*The Twenty-One Balloons*, 1948 Newbery Medal) got into a discussion with another boy while they were taking foot baths. They decided they'd take off in a balloon if they knew the earth were about to explode.

Barbara Cooney kept live chickens and took plants from her own garden to use as models for illustrating backgrounds in *Chanticleer and the Fox* (1959 Caldecott Medal).

Because of illness, Anna Sewell was mostly confined to her bed or the sofa while she wrote *Black Beauty*.

June 21

A boy wrote to Beverly Cleary stating he'd read *Dear Mr. Henshaw* (1984 Newbery Medal) straight through the first day he got the book and five times the following week.

Armstrong Sperry gave his acceptance speech for *Call It Courage* (1941 Newbery Medal) during a thunderstorm. He chanted Polynesian songs while so much rain fell that a canopy threatened to collapse under the weight of the water.

The Stinky Cheese Man and Other Fairly Stupid Tales (1993 Caldecott Honor Book) has more pages than the average picture book because creators Lane Smith and Jon Scieszka felt that timing and pace were essential to the humor.

June 22

After Patricia MacLachlan won the 1986 Newbery Medal for *Sarah, Plain and Tall*, she received a letter from a child that said, "I know you have to write a speech. Try, if you can, not to be boring."

The primary medium of Marcia Brown's three books that won the gold Caldecott Medal are all different: *Cinderella* (1955) is gouache, *Once a Mouse* (1962) is woodcuts, and *Shadow* (1983) is cut paper collage.

Although *The Cat in the Hat* and *Green Eggs and Ham* are the most popular of Dr. Seuss's books, neither was recognized by the Caldecott Committee.

June 23

Emily Neville's (*It's Like This, Cat*, 1964 Newbery Medal) father and dog both hated cats. She assumed they were right until she learned for herself that cats can be terrific.

Nicolas Mordvinoff was asleep when the mail carrier rang the doorbell to deliver a letter announcing *Finders Keepers* had won the 1952 Caldecott Medal. He had been dreaming of being in a boxing ring with a "huge, fierce-looking prizefighter."

Curious George had his start as a character named Zozo.

June 24

At various times Maia Wojciechowska (*Shadow of a Bull*, 1965 Newbery Medal) worked as a pro tennis player, a masseuse, and an undercover detective.

Allen Say didn't consciously model any of the people in *Grandfather's Journey* (1995 Caldecott Medal) on anyone he knew, except himself. He later realized the young woman who is supposed to be his mother looks similar to a girl he liked in middle school.

Moby Dick is considered to be one of the 100 most influential books.

June 25

 BORN ON THIS DAY:

Eric Carle, 1929

Elizabeth Orton Jones, 1910

George Orwell, 1903

Avi (*The True Confessions of Charlotte Doyle*, 1991 Newbery Honor Book and *Nothing But the Truth*, 1992 Newbery Honor Book) almost flunked out of high school during his first term, but continued to read "everything and anything."

The silver cup, the patchwork quilt, and the top in *Prayer for a Child* (1945 Caldecott Medal) all came from Elizabeth Orton Jones's memories.

Eric Carle, creator of *The Very Hungry Caterpillar*, owned only three books as a child: a Mickey Mouse book and a Flash Gordon book while he was in the United States, and a Max and Moritz and Struwelpeter book while he was in Germany.

George Orwell, the pen name of Eric Arthur Blair, composed his first poem at the age of four or five. Because he didn't yet know how to write, his mother wrote it down for him.

June 26

 BORN ON THIS DAY:

Walter Farley, 1922

Lynd Ward, 1905

Nancy Willard, 1936

Nancy Willard (*A Visit to William Blake's Inn*, 1982 Newbery Medal and Caldecott Honor Book) spent much of her childhood eavesdropping on a party line telephone. Her interest in inns grew from one of those overheard conversations.

Some of the staff at Houghton Mifflin gave Lynd Ward a copy of *The Biggest Bear* (1953 Caldecott Medal) bound in bearskin as a gift.

Walter Farley, author of the Black Stallion books, grew up in Syracuse, New York. He went to racetracks to be around horses.

June 27

Esther Forbes and Lynd Ward, author and illustrator of *Johnny Tremain* (1944 Newbery Medal), were born two days short of fourteen years apart.

Barbara Cooney's editor received the illustrations for *Ox-Cart Man* (1980 Caldecott Medal) in a mahogany box with an ox Cooney painted on the cover.

Lois Duncan suddenly felt old while autographing books when an "old, white-haired lady" told her she read Duncan's books while in high school.

June 28

 BORN ON THIS DAY:
Esther Forbes, 1891

Esther Forbes won a Pulitzer Prize for her biography of Paul Revere. The idea for *Johnny Tremain* (1944 Newbery Medal) grew from her research on Paul Revere.

Leo Dillon and Diane Dillon enjoyed illustrating *Why Mosquitoes Buzz in People's Ears* (1976 Caldecott Medal) because the manuscript didn't present the usual problems they have.

Mark Twain said that the early controversy over *Adventures of Huckleberry Finn* would "sell 25,000 copies for us sure."

June 29

Harold Keith purposely introduced new characters, a different setting, and a different element of the war in each chapter of *Rifles for Watie* (1958 Newbery Medal).

Two versions of picture book stories illustrated by Randolph Caldecott became Caldecott books: *Frog Went A-Courtin'* (1956 Caldecott Medal) and *The Three Jovial Huntsmen* (1974 Caldecott Honor Book).

Theodor Seuss Geisel (Dr. Seuss) said, "Adults are only obsolete children so to hell with them!"

June 30

Elizabeth Yates's research and persistence led to the discovery of several of Amos Fortune's papers that had been lost for 50 years.

As a child Dorothy Lathrop's (*Animals of the Bible*, 1938 Caldecott Medal) favorite Bible stories were those about animals.

The Mystery Writers of America present a small bust of Edgar Allan Poe—the Edgar Award—for excellence in mystery writing.

July 1

BORN ON THIS DAY:
Emily Arnold McCully, 1939

Adult critics objected to the death of Trinket in *Roller Skates* (1937 Newbery Medal) but children didn't.

Emily Arnold McCully originally intended *Mirette on the High Wire* (1993 Caldecott Medal) to be a biography of the daredevil Blondin.

As a child Rudyard Kipling was beaten and humiliated by the foster parents he stayed with for six years while his parents were in India. Eventually the abuse caused him to become temporarily blind and to have delusions.

July 2

BORN ON THIS DAY:
Jean Craighead George, 1919

Reader's Digest sent Jean Craighead George to Alaska to do research for an article on wolves. Her article was never published, but she used her research to write *Julie of the Wolves* (1973 Newbery Medal).

As a child, Trina Schart Hyman (*Saint George and the Dragon*, 1985 Caldecott Medal) was afraid to get shots until her mother told her getting a shot was like being pricked by the spindle of the spinning wheel in *Sleeping Beauty*.

Robinson Crusoe is based on the experiences of Alexander Selkirk who voluntarily spent four years alone on the island of Juan Fernandez because he objected to the conditions aboard a ship.

July 3

Jean Craighead George and John Schoenherr, author and illustrator of *Julie of the Wolves* (1973 Newbery Medal), were born sixteen years and three days apart.

Anatole (1957 Caldecott Honor Book) began as a bedtime story for Eve Titus's son Ricky in answer to his questions about the business world where his father worked.

The Raven and Other Poems by Edgar Allan Poe is considered one of the 100 most influential books.

July 4

BORN ON THIS DAY:
Nathaniel Hawthorne, 1804

As Eleanor Estes rose to give her acceptance speech for *Ginger Pye* (1952 Newbery Medal), her dress became caught under the leg of William Lipkind's (*Finders Keepers*, 1952 Caldecott Medal) chair. She fell but got up laughing.

Janet Stevens (*Tops and Bottoms*, 1996 Caldecott Honor Book) once designed fabric patterns for Hawaiian shirts.

Lewis Carroll told the story of Alice to the Liddell sisters while on a boat trip on July 4, 1862. Alice Liddell begged him to write the story down and *Alice's Adventures in Wonderland* was published three years later.

Nathaniel Hawthorne's name was actually spelled "Hathorne," but he added the "w" when he started writing.

Mark Twain's home town of Hannibal, Missouri declared July 4 to be Tom Sawyer Fence Painting Day during which a fence painting contest is held.

July 5

 BORN ON THIS DAY:
John Schoenherr, 1935

Ellen Raskin wanted to write a "bicentennial" book when she wrote *The Westing Game* (1979 Newbery Medal), so she used the song "America the Beautiful" for the clues in the book and a "melting pot" of different nationalities for the characters.

Several scenes in *Owl Moon* (1988 Caldecott Medal) are from John Schoenherr's farm where he went owling with his own children.

Lord of the Flies by William Golding is number forty-one on the Modern Library Board's list of 100 best novels published in the English language since 1900.

July 6

 BORN ON THIS DAY:
Dhan Mukerji, 1890

Gay-Neck: The Story of a Pigeon (1928 Newbery Medal) is based on author Dhan Mukerji's childhood.

Maurice Sendak based characters in *Outside over There* (1982 Caldecott Honor Book) on Fanny Brice as Baby Snooks, Eddie Cantor, and Sendak's sister.

Bernard Waber drew his comic crocodile Lyle after he discovered that he got more recognition from his art when he included a humorous twist.

July 7

Karen Hesse (*Out of the Dust*, 1998 Newbery Medal) said, "Winning a Newbery could give a person heart failure."

At one time, Virginia Lee Burton's (*The Little House*, 1943 Caldecott Medal) home was picked up and moved from the side of the main road back into an area with many apple trees.

Hans Christian Andersen's "The Ugly Duckling" is considered a symbol of his own life because he wasn't very good looking.

July 8

Hendrik Van Loon (*The Story of Mankind*, 1922 Newbery Medal) was known as "Uncle Hank" on shortwave radio during World War II.

Before he became an illustrator, some of Blair Lent's (*The Funny Little Woman*, 1973 Caldecott Medal) more unusual jobs included dressing mannequins (sometimes accidentally putting their clothes on backward), caring for penguins in a window display, and gutting chickens.

George Orwell submitted the manuscript for *1984* as "1948," the year he completed the writing.

July 9

 BORN ON THIS DAY:
Nancy Farmer, 1941

Nancy Farmer (*The Ear, the Eye, and the Arm*, 1995 Newbery Honor Book, and *A Girl Named Disaster*, 1997 Newbery Honor Book) once watched a circus veterinarian give an elephant an autopsy and was fascinated to discover the animal had two hearts.

Jerry Pinkney, illustrator of Caldecott Honor Books *Mirandy and Brother Wind* (1989), *The Talking Eggs* (1990), and *John Henry* (1995), didn't read much as a child, but as an adult he spends much time in libraries and owns a large collection of books.

The Runaway Bunny, one of the most popular books among children, was not selected as a Caldecott Medal winner or Honor Book.

While writing *Pinocchio*, Carlo Collodi was determined not to mention religion primarily because he, as a deeply religious man, didn't want to be irreverent.

July 10

 BORN ON THIS DAY:
Martin Provensen, 1916

Elizabeth Enright got the idea for *Thimble Summer* (1939 Newbery Medal) while she was watering her garden with water hauled in coffee cans, kettles, and any other container she could find.

Martin Provensen (*The Glorious Flight*, 1984 Caldecott Medal) was an amateur pilot.

Margaret Wise Brown encouraged Esphyr Slobodkina, author of *Caps for Sale*, to write her own books after she had illustrated several books written by others.

July 11

 BORN ON THIS DAY:
E. B. White, 1899

As children, prize fighter Jack Iman bullied Scott O'Dell (*Island of the Blue Dolphins*, 1961 Newbery Medal). As adults, O'Dell attended many of Iman's fights, hoping to see him beaten but had to wait a year before finally seeing Iman get knocked out.

Elwyn Brooks White (*Charlotte's Web*, 1953 Newbery Honor Book) didn't like the name his parents gave him, which is why he used his initials for his writing. When he attended Cornell University, his nickname became "Andy" in honor of the first university president, Andrew D. White.

The film *Madeline* includes incidents from all the Madeline books including *Madeline's Rescue* (1954 Caldecott Medal) and *Madeline* (1940 Caldecott Honor Book).

July 12

The dog that inspired *Shiloh* (1992 Newbery Medal) was renamed Clover.

Katherine Paterson said that *Bridge to Terabithia* (1978 Newbery Medal) reminds her of an unaccompanied flute solo in intricacy, density, and design.

As a child, Gerald McDermott (*Arrow to the Sun*, 1975 Caldecott Medal) acted in a radio show that dramatized folk tales and legends.

July 13

 BORN ON THIS DAY:
Marcia Brown, 1918

A Navajo medicine man said Ann Nolan Clark's (*Secret of the Andes*, 1953 Newbery Medal) writing was "as good as a Navajo could write," meaning that she wrote as if she herself were a Navajo.

Marcia Brown is the only illustrator to win three top Caldecott awards. She won with *Cinderella* in 1955, *Once a Mouse* in 1962, and *Shadow* in 1983.

When Charles Dickens visited the United States in 1842, people gave him a hero's welcome. People were just as happy to see him on his return visit in 1867.

July 14

 BORN ON THIS DAY:
Isaac Bashevis Singer, 1904

The paintings of Velasquez inspired Elizabeth Borton de Treviño to write *I, Juan de Pareja* (1966 Newbery Medal).

Isaac Singer wrote for the *Jewish Daily Forward* in Yiddish. This fact made Maurice Sendak's parents very proud when their son illustrated Singer's *Zlateh the Goat* (1967 Newbery Honor Book).

Duffy and the Devil (1974 Caldecott Medal), *Tom Tit Tot* (1966 Caldecott Honor Book), and *Rumplestiltskin* (1987 Caldecott Honor Book) are all versions of the same basic story.

July 15

 BORN ON THIS DAY:
Walter D. Edmonds, 1903
Clement Moore, 1779

The character of Jack Darby in *The Matchlock Gun* (1942 Newbery Medal) is loosely based on a man named Thomas Shepherd who told author Walter Edmonds a story about an incident involving a gun that happened in his family.

Of all the books Dr. Seuss created, only three were Caldecott Honor Books: *McElligot's Pool* (1948), *Bartholomew and the Oobleck* (1950), and *If I Ran the Zoo* (1951).

Clement Clarke Moore's niece anonymously submitted "A Visit from St. Nicholas" to the *Troy Sentinel* where the poem was published in 1823. More than 20 years passed before Moore acknowledged the fact that he wrote the poem.

July 16

 BORN ON THIS DAY:
Arthur Bowie Chrisman, 1889
Richard Egielski, 1952

Arthur Bowie Chrisman spent seven years writing *Shen of the Sea* (1926 Newbery Medal).

The Caldecott Committee didn't have Richard Egielski's phone number to call him when they selected *Hey, Al!* as the recipient of the 1987 Caldecott Medal. They called author Arthur Yorinks to get Egielski's number.

Charles Lutwidge Dodgson, better known as Lewis Carroll, wrote serious books on math as well as fantasy novels.

July 17

Meindert DeJong used himself as a model for Joe in *Along Came a Dog* (1959 Newbery Honor Book).

Chris Van Allsburg's wife posed for him while he drew the monkeys in *Jumanji* (1982 Caldecott Medal).

S. E. Hinton started writing *The Outsiders* when she was fifteen years old.

July 18

Many critics said children would never be able to understand the cowboy lingo in *Smoky the Cowhorse* (1927 Newbery Medal), but they were obviously wrong.

Kate Seredy (*Dobry*, 1935 Newbery Medal) saw the book *Hitty: Her First Hundred Years* (1930 Newbery Medal) on display and told herself, "You are a great artist, Dorothy Lathrop, but you wait . . . I am coming, too."

When Peter Spier's phone rang at 4:30 AM one day, his first thought was "My parents' house is on fire." Instead, he heard he'd won the 1978 Caldecott Medal for *Noah's Ark*.

July 19

Armstrong Sperry (*Call It Courage*, 1941 Newbery Medal) was married to Margaret Mitchell, author of *Gone with the Wind*.

A 1960 *Publishers Weekly* poll showed that *Charlotte's Web* (1953 Newbery Honor Book) is considered the best children's book written between 1930 and 1960.

When David Wiesner showed his editor the dummy book for *Tuesday* (1992 Caldecott Medal), she laughed, and then they "sat around making pig and frog noises for a while."

R. L. Stine, author of the Goosebumps series, once received a letter from a child saying, "I read forty of your books. They were all boring."

July 20

Jean Lee Latham used twenty pages of notes for *Carry on, Mr. Bowditch* (1956 Newbery Medal) and then relied on her imagination to fill out the rest of the book.

Uri Shulevitz (*The Fool of the World and the Flying Ship*, 1969 Caldecott Medal) spent his first four years in Warsaw. Two things he remembers from that time are a bomb killing approximately one-third of the people standing in a bread line with him and another bomb destroying the stairs to his apartment.

Mary Mapes Dodge, author of *Hans Brinker; Or the Silver Skates*, was appointed founder-editor of the long-running children's magazine *St. Nicholas*.

July 21

 BORN ON THIS DAY:
Ernest Hemingway, 1899

Lois Lowry's plane taking her to New York for a *Today* show appearance, after she won the 1990 Newbery Medal for *Number the Stars*, took off in a snowstorm. The plane had to land on an abandoned airstrip because it ran low on fuel after circling for so long in the inclement weather.

Mark Simont (*A Tree Is Nice*, 1957 Caldecott Medal) was always more interested in what his teachers looked like than in what they said.

Ernest Hemingway lost many early manuscripts when a trunk filled with his writing was forgotten on a train in France.

July 22

 BORN ON THIS DAY:
Margery Bianco, 1881

Because Mildred Taylor's (*Roll of Thunder, Hear My Cry*, 1977 Newbery Medal) writing seems so realistic, many people believe her works are autobiographical, but they aren't.

Margery Bianco (*Winterbound*, 1937 Newbery Honor Book) learned the names of most animals and birds before she learned the multiplication table.

Peggy Rathmann started *Officer Buckle and Gloria* (1996 Caldecott Medal) for a class assignment requiring that the illustrations tell part of the story.

July 23

Originally Louis Sachar didn't intend for Stanley in *Holes* (1999 Newbery Medal) to have the last name Yelnats. He simply didn't want to stop to think of a last name as he was writing, so he just used the first name spelled backward.

Carol Ryrie Brink's grandmother made comments and suggestions about the manuscript for *Caddie Woodlawn* (1936 Newbery Medal).

Paul O. Zelinsky (*Rapunzel*, 1998 Caldecott Medal) bought rapunzel seeds and his wife tended the plants on the roof deck of their apartment building. The plants bloomed the first year even though rapunzel usually doesn't bloom until the second year.

Editor Thomas Niles was so disappointed in the manuscript for *Little Women*, he almost didn't publish the book. He reconsidered after all the girls he gave the manuscript to read loved the story.

July 24

In the sequel to *Sounder* (1970 Newbery Medal), author William Armstrong gives the boy the name Moses Waters.

David Diaz (*Smoky Night*, 1995 Caldecott Medal) cites William Steig (*Sylvester and the Magic Pebble*, 1970 Caldecott Medal) as a great influence.

"Mark Twain" means two fathoms, or twelve feet.

July 25

Sid Fleischman spent ten years working on *The Whipping Boy* (1987 Newbery Medal). It originally began as a picture book.

Louis Blériot, the subject of *The Glorious Flight* (1984 Caldecott Medal) used the fortune he earned from inventing an automobile searchlight to develop his aircraft. His historic flight across the English Channel took place on July 25, 1909.

L. Frank Baum's first book was a textbook about chickens titled *The Book of Hamburgs* and published in 1886.

July 26

 BORN ON THIS DAY:
Jan Berenstain, 1923
Margaret Hodges, 1911

Krakow officials generously lent the original trumpet the trumpeters of Krakow used for hundreds of years for the 1929 Newbery Award ceremony. A Marine Corps bugler played the "Heynal," a traditional Polish theme, on the trumpet as Eric Kelly received the Medal for *The Trumpeter of Krakow*.

Margaret Hodges (*Saint George and the Dragon*, 1985 Caldecott Medal) adapted children's books for a radio program and then became a radio storyteller on a program that started out local and became national.

Stan Berenstain and Jan Berenstain started writing their Berenstain Bears books when they couldn't find enough humorous books for their children.

July 27

Hugh Lofting (*The Voyages of Dr. Dolittle*, 1923 Newbery Medal) thought books should have a "senile" category to go along with the "juvenile" category.

Robert Lawson (*Rabbit Hill*, 1945 Newbery Medal and *They Were Strong and Good*, 1941 Caldecott Medal) had a sign beside his driveway reading, "Please drive carefully on account of small animals."

While the children were playing the "jungle game" in *Jumanji* (1982 Caldecott Medal), a lion appeared, but lions live on the grasslands and the plains, not in jungles.

While ill in the South Pacific, Robert Louis Stevenson was too weak to hold a pen or even speak. He dictated his stories by using sign language.

July 28

 BORN ON THIS DAY:

Natalie Babbitt, 1932

Beatrix Potter, 1866

Natalie Babbitt (*Kneeknock Rise*, 1971 Newbery Medal) started her book career illustrating what her husband wrote. When he became too busy to write, she started writing in order to have something to illustrate.

After her father broke his leg, Virginia Lee Burton (*The Little House*, 1943 Caldecott Medal) cancelled a contract she had to become a dancer. While caring for him, she began painting and drawing again.

Beatrix Potter had two original Randolph Caldecott illustrations in her bedroom. She tried again and again to copy Caldecott's style but finally gave up in frustration.

July 29

 BORN ON THIS DAY:

Sharon Creech, 1945

A fortune cookie gave Sharon Creech the title of *Walk Two Moons* (1995 Newbery Medal). The fortune read, "Don't judge a man until you've walked two moons in his moccasins." She thought that finding an American Indian proverb in a Chinese fortune cookie in England was interesting.

To be accurate in his illustration of duck's bill, viewed from below as the duck flies, Robert McCloskey (*Make Way for Ducklings*, 1942 Caldecott Medal) wrapped a duck in a towel and placed it on a couch so that its head hung over the side. McCloskey then stretched out on the floor below the duck to sketch it.

When We Were Very Young by A. A. Milne was the third best-seller on the nonfiction list in 1925.

July 30

 BORN ON THIS DAY:

Emily Brontë, 1818

Mayor Fiorello La Guardia arrived at the funeral of Hendrik Van Loon (*The Story of Mankind*, 1922 Newbery Medal) in a car with sirens blaring—a day early. The following day, La Guardia arrived late and spent time during the funeral signing papers brought by special messenger.

Margaret Wise Brown (Golden MacDonald's real name) gave Leonard Weisgard a pocket watch to commemorate their winning the 1947 Caldecott Medal for *The Little Island*.

Emily Brontë based the character Heathcliff in *Wuthering Heights* on her brother Patrick Branwell Brontë.

July 31

 BORN ON THIS DAY:
Muriel Feelings, 1938

Editor May Massee asked Kate Seredy to write the story of her childhood in Hungary. Seredy spent two months working on the manuscript in longhand and then sent the manuscript to the editor without typing the pages. The manuscript became the book *The Good Master* (1936 Newbery Honor Book).

Muriel Feelings (*Jambo Means Hello*, 1975 Caldecott Honor Book and *Moja Means One*, 1972 Caldecott Honor Book) spent time working, through the United Nations, as an art teacher in Uganda.

In addition to writing and illustrating books, Shel Silverstein wrote songs such as "On the Cover of the Rolling Stone," sung by Dr. Hook and the Medicine Show, and "A Boy Named Sue," sung by Johnny Cash.

August 1

BORN ON THIS DAY:
Herman Melville, 1819

Walter D. Edmonds (*The Matchlock Gun*, 1942 Newbery Medal) said he considered declining the Newbery because he thought novelists should write and never make speeches. He decided to accept the award due to another of his philosophies: Never decline anything that doesn't cost anything.

Ezra Jack Keats once clipped pictures of a boy out of *Life* magazine. Twenty-two years later, the boy in the pictures became the inspiration for Peter in *The Snowy Day* (1963 Caldecott Medal).

Herman Melville was a close friend of Nathaniel Hawthorne, who may have given Melville the idea for *Moby Dick*.

August 2

BORN ON THIS DAY:
Holling Clancy Holling, 1900

It's Like This, Cat (1964 Newbery Medal) is credited with being one of the first "tough teen" books.

Holling Clancy Holling (*Paddle-to-the-Sea*, 1942 Caldecott Honor Book; *Minn of the Mississippi*, 1952 Newbery Honor Book; and *Seabird*, 1949 Newbery Honor Book) legally changed his name from Holling Clancy because his signature on his artwork looked as if it were the three names.

Richard Egielski (*Hey, Al!*, 1987 Caldecott Medal) didn't discover picture books until he was older than the usual picture book age.

After failing to find a publisher in America, Washington Irving, author of *The Legend of Sleepy Hollow*, went to Britain to be published. The British gave him many honorary degrees and medals for his work.

August 3

BORN ON THIS DAY:
Mary Calhoun, 1926

Katherine Paterson received a letter from a child praising *The Great Gilly Hopkins* (1979 Newbery Honor Book). This previously reluctant-reader wrote, "I love the book. I am on page 16." The child did finish the book—four times—and then read *Bridge to Terabithia* (1978 Newbery Medal).

Leo Dillon and Diane Dillon started illustrating *Ashanti to Zulu* (1977 Caldecott Medal) in a decorative style, but later changed the style to be more realistic.

Mary Calhoun's books about Katie John, set in her childhood home in Iowa, are based on the things she did and the thoughts she had while growing up.

August 4

Russell Freedman, as well as many others, was surprised when his nonfiction book *Lincoln: A Photobiography* won the 1988 Newbery Medal. He noted that, up to that point, only six nonfiction books had won the award and the last one had been thirty-two years prior. He also pointed out that all the nonfiction winners were biographies except for the first winner in 1922, *The Story of Mankind*.

A high school teacher suggested that John Steptoe (*The Story of Jumping Mouse*, 1985 Caldecott Honor Book and *Mufaro's Beautiful Daughters*, 1988 Caldecott Honor Book) visit

Harper publishers to see about an illustrating job. Harper published Steptoe's book *Stevie* when he was only nineteen years old.

Theodor Seuss Geisel (Dr. Seuss) said that he got his ideas on August fourth of every summer while in Uber Gletch in Switzerland, where he went to get his cuckoo clock repaired.

Mark Twain based the character Huck Finn on a boyhood friend named Tom Blankenship.

August 5

 BORN ON THIS DAY:
Maud Petersham, 1889
Ruth Sawyer, 1880

Ruth Sawyer based *Roller Skates* (1937 Newbery Medal) on a year in her life when her parents were abroad.

Maud Petersham told herself jingles, songs, and rhymes to keep from worrying so much about her son while he served in World War II. If she couldn't remember the exact words, she'd find the item in a book. Soon she had enough material for *The Rooster Crows* (1946 Caldecott Medal).

In the 1970s, many people wore buttons reading "Tolkien is hobbit-forming."

August 6

 BORN ON THIS DAY:
Barbara Cooney, 1917

In illustrating *Amos Fortune, Free Man* (1951 Newbery Medal), Nora Unwin visited many of the places and examined many of the things Amos Fortune found important such as his home, his church, and his tanning tools.

Whenever possible, Barbara Cooney (*Chanticleer and the Fox*, 1959 Caldecott Medal and *Ox-Cart Man*, 1980 Caldecott Medal) tried to use actual models and scenes—including plants, animals, places, and more—for her art.

A man told Rudyard Kipling about being stolen as a baby and growing up knowing only the language of his kidnappers. Kipling used this story as the basis for *Kim*.

August 7

 BORN ON THIS DAY:
Betsy Byars, 1928
Maia Wojciechowska, 1927

An article about swans in Betsy Byars's college alumni magazine sparked the idea for *The Summer of the Swans* (1971 Newbery Medal).

Maia Wojciechowska developed *Shadow of a Bull* (1965 Newbery Medal) from a short story into a book after she saw a girl she thought looked like an intellectual. Wojciechowska wrote the book with that girl in mind.

Dianne Snyder wanted to write a collection of Japanese folktales, but *The Boy of the Three-Year Nap* (1989 Caldecott Honor Book) became a book by itself.

August 8

 BORN ON THIS DAY:
Marjorie Kinnan Rawlings, 1896

Marjorie Kinnan Rawlings's (*The Secret River*, 1956 Newbery Honor Book) book *The Yearling* won the 1939 Pulitzer Prize for fiction.

While working on the illustrations for *Animals of the Bible* (1938 Caldecott Medal), Dorothy Lathrop had trouble with her animal models—they kept falling asleep.

For writing *Hamlet*, William Shakespeare earned what would be about five British pounds today.

August 9

While speaking at a school, Phyllis Reynolds Naylor overheard a child say, "*Seventy books, and she's never won the Newbery?*" Soon after, Naylor won the 1992 Newbery Medal for *Shiloh*.

In 1928, Laura Adams Armer (*Waterless Mountain*, 1932 Newbery Medal) produced a film titled *The Mountain Chant*. The film, depicting a Navajo ceremony, is the first to be filmed entirely in the original Native American language.

John Schoenherr's wife suggested he add the semi-hidden animals to the illustrations in *Owl Moon* (1988 Caldecott Medal).

August 10

Elizabeth Enright wrote *Thimble Summer* (1939 Newbery Medal) during a drought. Unlike the book, rain didn't come soon enough to save her own family's crops.

Maurice Sendak (*Where the Wild Things Are*, 1964 Caldecott Medal) said Randolph Caldecott is his favorite illustrator largely due to the organization of the books.

The first sequel to a successful novel was *The Further Adventures of Robinson Crusoe* in 1719.

August 11

Even before she wrote a book, Eleanor Estes (*Ginger Pye*, 1952 Newbery Medal) used to think about giving a Newbery acceptance speech to help her fall asleep.

Edgar d'Aulaire (*Abraham Lincoln*, 1940 Caldecott Medal) used the money he received from being injured in a Paris bus accident to move to the United States.

Robert Newton Peck, author of the Soup and Trig books, chose Fred Rogers of *Mister Rogers' Neighborhood* to be the best man at his wedding.

August 12

 BORN ON THIS DAY:
Ruth Stiles Gannett, 1923
Walter Dean Myers, 1937

Ruth Stiles Gannett spent two weeks writing *My Father's Dragon* (1949 Newbery Honor Book). Her stepmother, Ruth Chrisman Gannett, illustrated the book.

As a child growing up in Harlem, Walter Dean Myers (*Scorpions*, 1989 Newbery Honor Book; *Somewhere in the Darkness*, 1993 Newbery Honor Book; and *Harlem*, 1998 Caldecott Honor Book) lived near poet Langston Hughes, heard Josephine Baker singing at the neighborhood church, and saw Sugar Ray Robinson boxing with neighborhood children.

Art instructors told Diane Dillon (*Why Mosquitoes Buzz in People's Ears*, 1976 Caldecott Medal; and *Ashanti to Zulu*, 1977 Caldecott Medal) that she would never be successful as an artist because she was a woman.

Walt Whitman's *Leaves of Grass* originally received less-than-complimentary reviews. John

Greenleaf Whittier threw his copy of the book into the fireplace.

August 13

After the initial research was completed, Harold Keith spent five years writing *Rifles for Watie* (1958 Newbery Medal).

All the faces Marie Hall Ets drew in *Nine Days to Christmas* (1960 Caldecott Medal) were of people she knew. She wasn't prepared for the hurt feelings of the children she didn't show in the book.

"Dr." Seuss was not a doctor.

August 14

 BORN ON THIS DAY:
Alice Provensen, 1918

Patricia MacLachlan wrote *Sarah, Plain and Tall* (1986 Newbery Medal) for her mother who had Alzheimer's disease.

Bette Greene's (*Philip Hall Likes Me. I Reckon Maybe.*, 1975 Newbery Honor Book) family christened their boat *The Philip Hall*.

Alice Provensen (*The Glorious Flight*, 1984 Caldecott Medal) worked for Walter Lantz Studios, famous for the Woody Woodpecker cartoons, and Martin Provensen worked for Walt Disney Studios.

August 15

 BORN ON THIS DAY:
Leonard Baskin, 1922
Walter Crane, 1845

According to the attendees of the 1921 American Library Association Conference, if the Newbery Medal had existed one year earlier, *The Story of Doctor Dolittle* would have been the recipient. One of the book's sequels, *The Voyages of Doctor Dolittle*, received the 1923 Newbery Medal.

Leonard Baskin (*Hosie's Alphabet*, 1973 Caldecott Honor Book) was studying to become a rabbi like his father until age fourteen when he saw a sculptor in Macy's department store and began studying art instead.

As a boy, Walter Crane sketched a milkman's pony. The milkman traded a glass of milk for the drawing.

August 16

 BORN ON THIS DAY:
Beatrice Schenk de Regniers, 1914

Kate Seredy (*The White Stag*, 1938 Newbery Medal), didn't think about writing, only illustrating, until her editor suggested she try writing.

Beatrice Schenk de Regniers (*May I Bring a Friend?*, 1965 Caldecott Medal), along with Eva Moore, Mary Michaels White, and Jan Carr, selected poetry to be included in the book *Sing a Song of Popcorn* (Scholastic, 1988), which was illustrated by nine Caldecott Award-winning artists.

J. M. Barrie commissioned artist Sir George Frampton to make a statue of Peter Pan. In 1912, the statue was secretly erected in Kensington Gardens to make it look as if it had appeared by magic.

August 17

John O'Hara Cosgrave illustrated *Carry On, Mr. Bowditch* (1956 Newbery Medal), and his wife, Mary Silva Cosgrave, edited the book.

Louis Slobodkin (*Many Moons*, 1944 Caldecott Medal) enjoyed reading in elevators and was happy if an elevator got stuck between floors.

Lewis Carroll, a mathematician in addition to a writer, memorized *pi* to seventy-one decimal places.

August 18

 BORN ON THIS DAY:
Paula Danziger, 1944

The 1949 and 1950 Newbery Medal recipients, *King of the Wind* and *The Door in the Wall*, were both written by authors named Marguerite (Henry and de Angeli).

Peter Spier (*Noah's Ark*, 1978 Caldecott Medal) considered himself lucky to be earning a living with his hobby.

Paula Danziger grew up in a family that she says would be considered dysfunctional today, but then was "just the Danzigers."

August 19

When Cynthia Rylant finished *A Fine White Dust* (1987 Newbery Honor Book), she didn't ever want to write another novel because it was such hard work. Six years later, her novel *Missing May* won the 1993 Newbery Medal.

Robert McCloskey and Marc Simont (*A Tree Is Nice*, 1957 Caldecott Medal) shared an apartment while McCloskey worked on *Make Way for Ducklings* (1942 Caldecott Medal). Simont "didn't bat an eye" when McCloskey brought ducks to live with them and followed them around with a tissue to clean up the droppings.

Lois Duncan hung around with her brother's sailor friends to get ideas for stories, which she then sold to confession magazines in order to support herself.

August 20

Lois Lowry included one of her friend's most vivid memories—the shiny boots of the soldiers (easy to see from a child's perspective)—in *Number the Stars* (1990 Newbery Medal).

Harve Zemach (*Duffy and the Devil*, 1974 Caldecott Medal) won a Fulbright Scholarship to study at the University of Vienna where he met his future wife and collaborator, Margot Zemach.

Jules Verne based *20,000 Leagues Under the Sea* on the French submarine *Le Plongeur* and on the work of his friend who developed a steam-driven submarine.

August 21

 BORN ON THIS DAY:
Arthur Yorinks, 1953

As a child, Arthur Bowie Chrisman (*Shen of the Sea*, 1926 Newbery Medal) was disgusted by his unimaginative brother who couldn't "see" the stories Chrisman told him.

As a child, Arthur Yorinks (*Hey, Al!*, 1987 Caldecott Medal) was afraid of birds, in part because he saw Alfred Hitchcock's *The Birds*, and in part because of an aunt who used to let her bird fly around the house.

Marc Brown sometimes gets so involved with his work he forgets to eat and sleeps under his desk.

August 22

Jane Leslie Conly, daughter of Robert C. O'Brien (*Mrs. Frisby and the Rats of NIMH*, 1972 Newbery Medal), continued her father's story with *R-T, Margaret, and the Rats of NIMH* and *Rasco and the Rats of NIMH*. Conly's book *Crazy Lady!* was a 1994 Newbery Honor Book.

Ludwig Bemelmans once saw a line of girls and their teacher watching a dog retrieve an artificial leg from the Seine. That scene, slightly altered, became part of *Madeline's Rescue* (1954 Caldecott Medal).

P. L. Travers started writing *Mary Poppins* while recovering from an illness. Travers said the title character appeared in her imagination to amuse her.

August 23

Mari Sandoz (*The Horsecatcher*, 1958 Newbery Honor Book) was shot twice in hunting accidents before she turned fifteen.

The combination of Marcia Brown spending time drawing at the Bronx Zoo and a friend sending her a book of fables initiated the idea for *Once a Mouse* (1962 Caldecott Medal).

For a few years starting in the late 1960s, the Newcott and Caldeberry Awards were presented to books that were popular through word-of-mouth, without regard to awards and reviews.

August 24

Several Newbery winners are part of a series in which an earlier book was an Honor Book. Examples include Lloyd Alexander's *The High King*, 1969 and *The Black Cauldron*, 1966; Susan Cooper's *The Grey King*, 1976 and *The Dark Is Rising*, 1974; and Robin McKinley's *The Hero and the Crown*, 1985 and *The Blue Sword*, 1983.

As a child, Gene Zion (*All Falling Down*, 1952 Caldecott Honor Book) often tried to finish all the books he had checked out of the library before he went home.

Shel Silverstein would have preferred being a good baseball player or a hit with the girls to being a good artist.

August 25

 BORN ON THIS DAY:
Lane Smith, 1959

Ellen Raskin (*The Westing Game*, 1979 Newbery Medal) said at the awards banquet in Dallas, ". . . what better place to celebrate about money and millionaires than Texas?"

Louis Sachar said he felt as if he let down the Newbery Committee by not screaming when he heard the news that he had won the 1999 Medal for *Holes*.

A "D" on a math paper made fourth-grader Lane Smith (*The Stinky Cheese Man and Other Fairly Stupid Tales*, 1993 Caldecott Honor Book) decide to become an artist when he grew up.

Eric Knight, author of *Lassie Come Home*, wanted to be a painter but discovered he was color-blind.

August 26

After hearing she had won the 1973 Newbery Medal for *Julie of the Wolves*, Jean Craighead George washed a load of clean clothes, put the book she was reading in the refrigerator, and served a guest an open can of dog food.

David Macaulay separated his acceptance speech into four mini-speeches, similar to the format of *Black and White* (1991 Caldecott Medal).

Johann Wyss originally told the story of *Swiss Family Robinson* to his sons. The story is based on a Russian sea captain's report of the discovery of a Swiss pastor and his family who'd been shipwrecked on an island near New Guinea.

August 27

 BORN ON THIS DAY:
Arlene Mosel, 1921
Suzanne Fisher Staples, 1945

Suzanne Fisher Staples (*Shabanu: Daughter of the Wind*, 1990 Newbery Honor Book) traveled with Indira Gandhi during one political campaign.

Arlene Mosel's (*The Funny Little Woman*, 1973 Caldecott Medal) mother frequently read fairy tales to her daughter.

Robert Louis Stevenson based the character Long John Silver on a close friend, W. E. Henley, who had lost a foot.

August 28

 BORN ON THIS DAY:
Roger Duvoisin, 1904
Brian Pinkney, 1961
Allen Say, 1937

E. B. White's contract for *Charlotte's Web* (1953 Newbery Honor Book) had a clause stating that the publisher would hold any royalties over $7,500 a year in a trust account. White joked that they kept the money "in a sock somewhere."

Roger Duvoisin said illustrating *White Snow, Bright Snow* (1948 Caldecott Medal) was easy because it was "only snow on a white page."

As a child, Brian Pinkney (*The Faithful Friend*, 1996 Caldecott Honor Book) had a miniature studio in a walk-in closet similar to the studio of his father, Caldecott Honor Book award-winner Jerry Pinkney.

In his acceptance speech for *Grandfather's Journey* (1994 Caldecott Medal), Allen Say mentioned that the first Caldecott book (*Animals of the Bible*, 1938) was published in the year of his birth.

August 29

 BORN ON THIS DAY:
Karen Hesse, 1952

Karen Hesse's *Out of the Dust* (1998 Newbery Medal) is the only Newbery book that tells a detailed story in free verse.

David Wisniewski (*Golem*, 1997 Caldecott Medal) and his wife founded a puppet theater troupe, which won the Henson Foundation grant in 1984 and again in 1985. The grant was established by Muppet creator Jim Henson.

Edgar Allan Poe submitted the manuscript of "The Raven" in person at the offices of *Graham's Magazine*. The magazine didn't purchase the poem but took up a collection and gave Poe $15.00 because he looked so desperate for money. The poem later sold to the *New York Mirror* for $10.00, and Poe had to wait more than a year to get the money.

August 30

 BORN ON THIS DAY:

Jean de Brunhoff, 1925

Virginia Lee Burton, 1909

Sesyle Joslin, 1929

Mary Shelley, 1797

Russell Freedman (*Lincoln: A Photobiography*, 1988 Newbery Medal) once worked as a publicity writer for network television shows, including *Father Knows Best*.

Virginia Lee Burton's (*The Little House*, 1943 Caldecott Medal) first attempt at writing was a book about a particle of dust. "Everyone" rejected it—even her four-year-old son who fell asleep when she read it to him.

What Do You Say, Dear? (1959 Caldecott Honor Book) grew from a game Sesyle Joslin played with her children.

Jean de Brunhoff died when his son Laurent was only 12 years old. Even then, Laurent wanted to continue his father's stories about Babar.

The idea for Mary Shelley's *Frankenstein* grew from a dream.

August 31

Sid Fleischman (*The Whipping Boy*, 1987 Newbery Medal) said his children didn't get hand-me-down clothes; they got hand-me-down typewriters.

Nonny Hogrogian listened to Scottish music while she worked on *Always Room for One More* (1966 Caldecott Medal).

The Adventures of Tom Sawyer, first published in 1876, broke with tradition by having a hero who was neither "good" nor learned a lesson from being "bad."

September 1

The only story Patricia MacLachlan (*Sarah, Plain and Tall*, 1986 Newbery Medal) remembers writing before age 35 was a school assignment. The entire story, including "THE END," was twelve words long.

Ludwig Bemelmans (*Madeline's Rescue*, 1954 Caldecott Medal) named his character after the woman he married in November 1935: Madeline Freund.

As children, Beatrix Potter and her brother dissected dead animals they found and tried to put their skeletons back together, sometimes successfully.

September 2

 BORN ON THIS DAY:
Elizabeth Borton de Treviño, 1904

Elizabeth Borton de Treviño (*I, Juan de Pareja*, 1966 Newbery Medal) contracted malaria at age six. During her recovery, she read everything she could find about slaves. Her interest in slaves remained with her through adulthood.

So many people said to Paul Zelinsky "I loved your book about Rapunzel," (when they meant *Rumplestiltskin* [1987 Caldecott Honor Book]) that he decided to do the book *Rapunzel* (1998 Caldecott Medal).

Bruce Degen, illustrator of the Magic School Bus series, knew he was a success when children asked him if he were *the* Bruce Degen.

September 3

Although he wanted to use only his personal experiences, Dhan Mukerji had to rely on the experiences of other pigeon trainers to complete *Gay-Neck, the Story of a Pigeon* (1928 Newbery Medal).

An emotionally-disturbed child who had never spoken asked, "Can I have that book?" after someone read *Where the Wild Things Are* (1964 Caldecott Medal) to her.

The Story of Ferdinand created much controversy because some critics called the book communist, fascist, or pacifist propaganda. Author Munro Leaf said Ferdinand was "just a superior soul" who showed "strength of character."

September 4

Laura Adams Armer based *Waterless Mountain* (1932 Newbery Medal) on the experiences of her son, Austin.

William Pène du Bois (*The Twenty-One Balloons*, 1948 Newbery Medal) never tested a book on children before it was published for fear the children would be bored.

While out birding with her father, Jane Yolen's daughter, Heidi, said she thought *Owl Moon* would win the 1988 Caldecott Medal. It did.

September 5

 BORN ON THIS DAY:
Paul Fleischman, 1952

Paul Fleischman was in the dentist's chair when the call about winning the 1989 Newbery for *Joyful Noise* came to his home. When he called home, his child told him about the "New baby." Fleischman said he hadn't realized they were planning a third child.

Donald Hall heard the story of *Ox-Cart Man* (1980 Caldecott Medal) from his cousin Paul

Fenton who had heard the story as a boy from "an old man" who had also heard the story from "an old man."

Lewis Carroll wrote most of the poems in the books about Alice as parodies of poems or popular songs.

September 6

Cornelia Meigs (*Invincible Louisa*, 1934 Newbery Medal) also wrote under the name Adair Alden.

Genevieve Foster spent three years working on *George Washington's World* (1942 Newbery Honor Book).

Illustrator Leonard Weisgard gave Margaret Wise Brown a box full of gold Caldecott Medal stickers to commemorate their work on *The Little Island* (1947 Caldecott Medal). Brown used the stickers on the dummies of her works in-progress.

September 7

 BORN ON THIS DAY:
Elmer Hader, 1889

During filming of the movie based on *Zlateh the Goat* (1967 Newbery Honor Book), the barn was so hot that the goat kept panting. The final version of the movie has the film speed slowed to make the goat seem more tranquil.

The heavy snowfall of 1947 inspired Berta Hader and Elmer Hader to write and illustrate the book *The Big Snow* (1949 Caldecott Medal).

The Library Committee at Concord, Massachusetts decided *Adventures of Huckleberry Finn* would "endanger the morals of the young."

September 8

Authorities at the Metropolitan Museum of Art were reluctant to give E. L. Konigsburg the information she needed for *From the Mixed-up Files of Mrs. Basil E. Frankweiler* (1968 Newbery Medal). She resorted to "snooping" to find out what she wanted.

Chris Van Allsburg (*Jumanji*, 1982 Caldecott Medal and *The Polar Express*, 1986 Caldecott Medal) says he steals his ideas from neighborhood kids, buys them by mail order, or has them beamed to him from outer space.

Some librarians drew diapers on Mickey in Maurice Sendak's book *In the Night Kitchen* (1971 Caldecott Honor Medal).

September 9

A book about Chesapeake Bay, given to her son by her sister, inspired Katherine Paterson to set *Jacob Have I Loved* (1981 Newbery Medal) in that area.

Margery Bianco's book *Winterbound* was a 1937 Newbery Honor Book, but she is better known as the author of *The Velveteen Rabbit*.

Trina Schart Hyman (*Saint George and the Dragon*, 1985 Caldecott Medal) often works so late that her dogs and cats fall asleep in a circle around her drawing board.

September 10

James Daugherty (*Daniel Boone*, 1940 Newbery Medal) went to high school in Washington, D.C., while his father worked for the Department of Agriculture. The Daughertys also lived in London while James's father was there representing the United States.

As a boy, Lynd Ward (*The Biggest Bear*, 1953 Caldecott Medal) hunted squirrels, rabbits, and birds. He ran into a bear one day but was smart enough to know that shooting it with his .22 would only wound it.

A biographer wrote that Hans Christian Andersen was a "crybaby."

September 11

 BORN ON THIS DAY:
O. Henry, 1862

Hendrik Van Loon (*The Story of Mankind*, 1922 Newbery Medal) created "Hendrik Van Loon's Wide World Game" in 1933.

Arthur Yorinks (*Hey, Al!*, 1987 Caldecott Medal) calls himself a "dogaholic."

O. Henry spent three years in jail for embezzling money while working as a bank clerk. He spent much of his time in prison writing.

September 12

The first illustration Will James (*Smoky the Cowhorse*, 1927 Newbery Medal) sold was a drawing of Smoky. *Sunset* magazine bought the drawing for $25.00.

After winning the 1976 Caldecott Medal for *Why Mosquitoes Buzz in People's Ears*, Leo Dillon and Diane Dillon set out to do the best book they'd ever done. They just happened to be working on *Ashanti to Zulu* at the time (1977 Caldecott Medal).

Charles Dickens rarely did any rewriting early in his career. Many of his published books are first drafts.

September 13

 BORN ON THIS DAY:
Roald Dahl, 1916

At age nine or ten, Mildred Taylor (*Roll of Thunder, Hear My Cry*, 1977 Newbery Medal) decided to write books about ordinary African American people.

The mother of Katherine Milhous (*The Egg Tree*, 1951 Caldecott Medal) pawned her wedding ring to raise the money to send her daughter to art school.

Roald Dahl, author of *Charlie and the Chocolate Factory* and *James and the Giant Peach*, grew up in a boarding school where the methods of discipline bordered on abuse.

September 14

 BORN ON THIS DAY:
William H. Armstrong, 1914
Diane Goode, 1949
John Steptoe, 1950

Sounder (1970 Newbery Medal) has been criticized for its supposed dehumanization of African American characters because William Armstrong named neither the boy nor his parents; others say not naming the characters universalized them.

As a child, Diane Goode (*When I Was Young in the Mountains*, 1983 Caldecott Honor Book) frequently visited museums in Europe. The paintings of the old masters especially caught her attention.

John Steptoe's (*The Story of Jumping Mouse*, 1985 Caldecott Honor Book and *Mufaro's Beautiful Daughters*, 1988 Caldecott Honor Book) painting and drawing didn't fit into his neighborhood in Brooklyn, New York where "slick talk, slick clothes," and playing basketball were more common.

Jack London's mother was an astrologer and his father never held a steady job.

September 15

 BORN ON THIS DAY:

James Fenimore Cooper, 1789

Robert McCloskey, 1914

Marjorie Kinnan Rawlings had hoped to make *The Secret River* (1956 Newbery Honor Book) longer, but she died before she could rewrite it. The book, in its original length, was published two years after her death.

Robert McCloskey (*Make Way for Ducklings*, 1942 Caldecott Medal and *Time of Wonder*, 1958 Caldecott Medal) married the daughter of Ruth Sawyer (*Roller Skates*, 1937 Newbery Medal). McCloskey and Sawyer collaborated on *Journey Cake, Ho!*, a 1954 Caldecott Honor Book.

The Alan Alda character, Dr. "Hawkeye" Pierce, in *M*A*S*H* got his nickname from the book *The Last of the Mohicans* by James Fenimore Cooper.

September 16

 BORN ON THIS DAY:

Thomas Handforth, 1897

H. A. Rey, 1898

The FBI investigated Phyllis Reynolds Naylor (*Shiloh*, 1992 Newbery Medal) for writing letters to United States senators protesting the imprisonment of a Korean poet. The FBI closed the case when they discovered that Naylor is an avid letter-writer.

Thomas Handforth based the characters in *Mei Li* (1939 Caldecott Medal) on the neighbors he had while living in China. The real Mei Li had been left on the doorstep of a missionary home. Igo and the thrush were his own pets.

H. A. Rey may have been inspired to create the Curious George books while he was growing up near a zoo. He spent much of his time at the zoo drawing.

September 17

 BORN ON THIS DAY:

Elizabeth Enright, 1909

Elizabeth Enright's (*Thimble Summer*, 1939 Newbery Medal) father was a political cartoonist, and her mother was an illustrator.

Clare Turlay Newberry, author/illustrator of four Caldecott Honor books about cats, wanted to be a portrait painter, but was more successful when her work reflected her life-long fascination with cats.

At *Black Beauty* author Anna Sewell's funeral, all bearing reins were removed from the horses in the funeral train, just as Sewell had requested before her death.

September 18

The story of *Ginger Pye* (1952 Newbery Medal) is based on a dog that author Eleanor Estes had as a child.

Donald Crews wrote and illustrated *Freight Train* (1979 Caldecott Honor Book) from his memories of traveling from New Jersey to Florida to visit his grandparents' farm for summer vacation.

Dr. Seuss thought *The Cat in the Hat* would take him a week or two to write, but he spent well over a year on the book.

September 19

BORN ON THIS DAY:
Rachel Field, 1894
William Golding, 1911

Author Rachel Field and illustrator Dorothy Lathrop found the six-and-one-half-inch doll that inspired *Hitty: Her First Hundred Years* (1930 Newbery Medal) in an antique store. Neither had enough money to purchase the doll individually, so they pooled their money to buy the doll together.

Don Wood (*King Bidgood's in the Bathtub*, 1986 Caldecott Honor Book) said some of his paintings contain one or two cat hairs because his cat named Gizmo kept him company while he worked.

William Golding wrote much of *Lord of the Flies* in class while he was a teacher.

September 20

BORN ON THIS DAY:
Miska Petersham, 1888

Beverly Cleary (*Dear Mr. Henshaw*, 1984 Newbery Medal) had difficulty learning how to read, but once she did, she quickly learned to love books.

Miska Petersham's (*The Rooster Crows*, 1946 Caldecott Medal) birth name was Petrezselyem Mihaly. He changed it because few people could pronounce his real name.

Ernest Hemingway's *The Old Man and the Sea* won the Pulitzer Prize for fiction in 1953.

September 21

The town in *Onion John* (1960 Newbery Medal) is based on Hope, New Jersey, where author Joseph Krumgold was living at the time he wrote the book.

In 1977, William Steig's *The Amazing Bone* was a Caldecott Honor Book and his *Abel's Island* was a Newbery Honor Book.

Rudyard Kipling became so famous, many people didn't cash the checks Kipling sent them because his autograph was so valuable.

September 22

Jerry Spinelli's *Maniac Magee* (1991 Newbery Medal) is based in part on a friend who grew up in an orphanage. The friend ran miles to get wherever he needed.

Peggy Rathmann spent four years revising *Officer Buckle and Gloria* (1996 Caldecott Medal) after the publisher accepted the manuscript.

Jonathan Swift wrote *Gulliver's Travels* to poke fun at the absurdities in English politics.

September 23

While Jean Craighead George was in Alaska doing research on wolves, her son pointed out a small child walking into the wilderness near Barrow. That child became the basis for *Julie of the Wolves* (1973 Newbery Medal).

During the filming of the movie based on the 1967 Newbery Honor Book, *Zlateh the Goat*, the goat frequently panicked and the child actor frequently cried and whined from being hot and exhausted.

Maurice Sendak based the five goblin babies in *Outside over There* (1982 Caldecott Honor Book) on the Dionne quintuplets.

September 24

 BORN ON THIS DAY:
L. Leslie Brooke, 1862

In 1979, the year after *Bridge to Terabithia* won the Newbery Medal, author Katherine Paterson's book *The Great Gilly Hopkins* was the only Newbery Honor Book.

Peter Sis (*Starry Messenger*, 1997 Caldecott Honor Book and *Tibet: Through the Red Box*, 1999 Caldecott Honor Book) once wrote to Maurice Sendak, not expecting a letter in return. Sendak didn't send him a letter but called him on the telephone instead.

The father of L. Leslie Brooke frequently recited a poem about Johnny Crow's garden and would make up a verse about what happened to any animal his sons suggested. Leslie continued the tradition with his own children. His wife is the one who suggested he write a book.

September 25

Cynthia Rylant (*Missing May*, 1993 Newbery Medal) didn't enter a library until she started college.

E. B. White once wrote to his editor, saying he thought *Charlotte's Web* (1953 Newbery Honor Book) would take forever to finish, but he completed the manuscript less than a year later.

The first time Ed Young (*Lon Po Po*, 1990 Caldecott Medal) visited the offices of Harper and Row, the guard directed him to the freight elevator thinking that Young was a delivery person.

September 26

Nancy Willard (*A Visit to William Blake's Inn*, 1982 Newbery Medal and Caldecott Honor Book) constructed an "inn" from grocery cartons, but her cat jumped into a box and destroyed the structure. A friend made a similar structure out of wood for her.

David Wiesner depicted himself as the man having a snack in *Tuesday* (1992 Caldecott Medal) because he wanted to be in the middle of the story.

J. M. Barrie is the first person known to use the name Wendy. A childhood friend had nicknamed Barrie Fwendy-Wendy, so he dropped the Fwendy and came up with the name Wendy for the character in his works about Peter Pan.

September 27

 BORN ON THIS DAY:
Paul Goble, 1933
Nicolas Mordvinoff, 1911
Bernard Waber, 1924

Lois Lowry based *Number the Stars* (1990 Newbery Medal) on a friend's childhood experiences. The friend, named Annelise, attended the awards banquet.

Paul Goble (*The Girl Who Loved Wild Horses*, 1979 Caldecott Medal) has been adopted into the Yakima and Sioux American Indian tribes.

As a child, Nicolas Mordvinoff (*Finders Keepers*, 1952 Caldecott Medal) was often scolded for making "silly drawings" instead of doing his schoolwork. At age five, he was already editing and illustrating a newspaper he wrote phonetically.

Bernard Waber's family moved frequently when he was a child. He adapted quickly as long as a library and a movie theater were within roller skating distance.

September 28

The Dark Frigate (1924 Newbery Medal) and *The Slave Dancer* (1974 Newbery Medal) have both been compared to *Treasure Island*. Note that the two Newbery Medal-winning books were published exactly fifty years apart.

Meindert DeJong wrote the place descriptions for *The Wheel on the School* (1955 Newbery Medal) entirely from his childhood memories. He didn't return to Holland until 1962.

Alice Provensen's and Martin Provensen's (*The Glorious Flight*, 1984 Caldecott Medal) fascination with airplanes began with the flying circuses they'd seen in the Midwest.

September 29

A Navajo medicine man, commenting on the work of Laura Adams Armer (*Waterless Mountain*, 1932 Newbery Medal), said, "The white woman paints strong medicine."

Maurice Sendak's editor once accidentally called him "Max" Sendak, like the boy in *Where the Wild Things Are* (1964 Caldecott Medal).

Leo Dillon and Diane Dillon are the only illustrators to win back-to-back Caldecotts. They won for *Why Mosquitoes Buzz in People's Ears* in 1976 and *Ashanti to Zulu* in 1977.

September 30

 BORN ON THIS DAY:
    Edgar d'Aulaire, 1898
    Alvin Tresselt, 1916

During his acceptance speech, William Pène du Bois admitted that he was mean to have made Professor Sherman speak before a large audience in *The Twenty-One Balloons* (1948 Newbery Medal).

Edgar d'Aulaire's (*Abraham Lincoln*, 1940 Caldecott Medal) maternal grandfather fought in the Civil War on the side of the North, even though he had a plantation in the Southwest.

Alvin Tresselt (*White Snow, Bright Snow*, 1948 Caldecott Medal) was the editor of *Humpty Dumpty's Magazine* from 1952 to 1965.

The first volume of *Little Women* was published on September 30, 1868.

October 1

A 1976 *Publishers Weekly* survey of people directly involved with children's books shows that *Island of the Blue Dolphins* (1961 Newbery Medal) is tenth on the list of best children's books written in America.

David Wisniewski (*Golem*, 1997 Caldecott Medal) attended the Ringling Brothers and Barnum & Bailey Circus Clown College. He performed with the circus for two seasons.

In October 1990, an early draft of the manuscript for *Adventures of Huckleberry Finn* was found in a steamer trunk in the attic of a house in Los Angeles. The manuscript contained much material that Mark Twain had deleted before the book was published.

October 2

Hugh Lofting (*The Voyages of Dr. Dolittle*, 1923 Newbery Medal) married three times; he was widowed early in both of his first two marriages.

Rachel Field died before Elizabeth Orton Jones even started the illustrations for *Prayer for a Child* (1945 Caldecott Medal).

The full title of *Kidnapped* is *Kidnapped, being memoirs of the adventures of David Balfour in the year 1751: how he was kidnapped and cast away; his sufferings in a desert isle; his journey in the Wild Highlands; his acquaintance with Alan Breck Stewart and other notorious Highland Jacobites; with all that he suffered at the hands of his uncle Ebenezer Balfour of Shaws, falsely so-called: written by himself, and now set forth by Robert Louis Stevenson.*

October 3

In October 1916, Elizabeth Coatsworth (*The Cat Who Went to Heaven*, 1931 Newbery Medal) first heard the legend of the painter and his cat. She didn't write the story until twelve years later.

In each illustration in *Ashanti to Zulu* (1977 Caldecott Medal), Leo Dillon and Diane Dillon tried to show a man, woman, and child in costume; a home; an artifact or type of work; and an animal.

John Newbery had to sell medicines as well as books to make a living. He combined his two professions and wrote about remedies for various ailments from toothaches to smallpox.

October 4

 BORN ON THIS DAY:
Karen Cushman, 1941
Robert Lawson, 1892
Donald Sobol, 1924
Edward Stratemeyer, 1862

Karen Cushman (*The Midwife's Apprentice*, 1996 Newbery Medal) started to write for herself the day her daughter started filling out college applications.

Robert Lawson wrote *They Were Strong and Good* (1941 Caldecott Medal) to promote interest and pride in ancestors. He wanted children to beg parents and grandparents for more stories.

Encyclopedia Brown creator Donald Sobol wanted to be a tenor, a sculptor, or a baseball player, but was tone deaf, discovered sculptors had to walk uptown for hot water, and couldn't hit a curve ball.

The Stratemeyer Syndicate produced many series books including the Hardy Boys, Nancy Drew, Tom Swift, the Bobbsey Twins, and more. Edward Stratemeyer wrote the outlines and edited many of the earlier books. He even wrote the first Bobbsey Twins book himself.

October 5

 BORN ON THIS DAY:
Gene Zion, 1913

James Daugherty (*Daniel Boone*, 1940 Newbery Medal) painted camouflage colors on ships during World War I. He said it was good experience for a mural painter.

Gene Zion and Margaret Bloy Graham, author and illustrator of *All Falling Down* (1952 Caldecott Honor Medal), were husband and wife who collaborated on some projects and worked separately on others.

Theodor Seuss Geisel saved his real name for writing serious work and wrote under the name Dr. Seuss for his more humorous material.

October 6

 BORN ON THIS DAY:
Elizabeth Janet Gray, 1902

At age thirteen, Elizabeth Janet Gray (*Adam of the Road*, 1943 Newbery Medal) received $2.00 for her first published story. The letter of acceptance began "Dear Mrs. Gray . . . ."

Of his own books, William Steig liked *Sylvester and the Magic Pebble* (1970 Caldecott Medal) and *Abel's Island* (1977 Newbery Honor Book) the best because he remembered doing them with excitement.

After the death of his daughter Josephine, Rudyard Kipling temporarily stopped writing for children.

October 7

Katherine Paterson (*Bridge to Terabithia*, 1978 Newbery Medal and *Jacob Have I Loved*, 1981 Newbery Medal) called herself a dreamer as a child but never envisioned seeing a book she wrote with a Newbery Medal on the cover, even though she read the Newbery books.

Sorche Nic Leodhas (*Always Room for One More*, 1966 Caldecott Medal) was ill as a child and didn't go to school. The classes she had at home were more difficult than school classes. She only had classes until 1:00 P.M., but she had classes six days a week.

Robinson Crusoe became the first novel to be serialized. *The Original London Post* printed the first installment of the pirated copy on October 7, 1719.

Edgar Allan Poe died on October 7, 1849. His epitaph reads "Quoth the Raven nevermore."

October 8

 BORN ON THIS DAY:
Faith Ringgold, 1930
R. L. Stine, 1943

Elizabeth George Speare (*The Witch of Blackbird Pond*, 1959 Newbery Medal and *The Bronze Bow*, 1962 Newbery Medal) couldn't remember liking history as a child, but she became interested when she realized her characters live in historical times.

Since Faith Ringgold (*Tar Beach*, 1992 Caldecott Honor Book) frequently suffered from asthma as a child, she spent time drawing and painting.

At age nine, R. L. Stine, author of the Goosebumps books, found an old typewriter and used it to type joke books.

October 9

Ellen Raskin knew she needed sixteen characters for *The Westing Game* (1979 Newbery Medal) so she went to what she called her "swipe file" (files of pictures cut from magazines) and selected sixteen of them for her characters.

Marcia Brown was concerned that *Shadow* (1983 Caldecott Medal) might not be accepted for publication, first, because she is a white woman and the book is about an African subject, and second, because the book was going to be expensive to print.

A 1976 *Publishers Weekly* survey of librarians, teachers, authors, and publishers selected *The Adventures of Tom Sawyer* as the third best children's book published in America and *Adventures of Huckleberry Finn* as the fifth best.

October 10

As a child, Elizabeth Enright (*Thimble Summer*, 1939 Newbery Medal) drew on anything she could find: a chalkboard, school books, the sidewalk, and even her knees.

Before starting to work on *Rapunzel* (1998 Caldecott Medal), Paul O. Zelinsky studied turrets and cupolas on buildings. When a wig stand holding a long blonde wig was suddenly placed in a window across the street from him, he knew he was meant to create the book.

Louisa May Alcott based the character of Jo in *Little Women* on herself.

October 11

 **BORN ON THIS DAY:**
Russell Freedman, 1929

Russell Freedman was born exactly 35 years after Eleanor Roosevelt. The biography written by Freedman, *Eleanor Roosevelt: A Life of Discovery*, was a 1994 Newbery Honor Book.

As soon as 100,000 copies of *Charlotte's Web* (1953 Newbery Honor Book) had been printed, the publisher presented a leatherbound copy of it to author E. B. White.

While working on *Outside over There* (1982 Caldecott Honor Book), Maurice Sendak listened only to the music of Mozart.

October 12

Patricia MacLachlan's fortune cookie message at lunch, just before she heard about winning the 1986 Newbery for *Sarah, Plain and Tall*, read, "Your talents will soon be recognized."

Arlene Mosel's (*The Funny Little Woman*, 1973 Caldecott Medal) two daughters each became librarians: one a law librarian and the other a children's librarian.

The Little Golden Books were first published in 1942. By 1955, more than 500 million copies had sold.

October 13

Maia Wojciechowska (*Shadow of a Bull*, 1965 Newbery Medal) became interested in bullfighting during visits to Spain.

Leonard Weisgard (*The Little Island*, 1947 Caldecott Medal) said he learned to illustrate picture books primarily by listening to Margaret Wise Brown.

Louise Fatio (*The Happy Lion*) and Roger Duvoisin (*White Snow, Bright Snow*, 1948 Caldecott Medal) were married.

October 14

 *BORN ON THIS DAY:*
Lois Lenski, 1893

Lois Lenski (*Strawberry Girl*, 1946 Newbery Medal) started her career illustrating books written by others yet still tried to give each book its own character. She gradually began writing her own material.

At age ten, David Macaulay (*Black and White*, 1991 Caldecott Medal) won a national handwriting award in England.

The Secret Garden grew out of a feeling Frances Hodgson Burnett had when she heard that the new owners of her former home had converted into a vegetable garden the rose garden she'd carefully raised out of an overgrown patch.

October 15

As a child, Beverly Cleary's (*Dear Mr. Henshaw*, 1984 Newbery Medal) class loved *Smoky the Cowhorse* (1927 Newbery Medal) but wasn't much interested in *Gay-Neck: The Story of a Pigeon* (1928 Newbery Medal).

Donald Hall's (*Ox-Cart Man*, 1980 Caldecott Medal) mother read poetry to him as a child. His grandfather recited poetry from memory.

In 1897, L. Frank Baum published his book *Mother Goose in Prose*, illustrated by Maxfield Parrish. The last story in the book introduced a farm girl named Dorothy, who would appear again in *The Wizard of Oz*.

October 16

And Now Miguel (1954 Newbery Medal) began as a film that Joseph Krumgold made for overseas distribution. The film has been translated into at least fifteen languages, and Universal Pictures made it into a movie in 1966.

While Barbara Cooney was ill, she read from Chaucer's *Canterbury Tales* which led to her idea for *Chanticleer and the Fox* (1959 Caldecott Medal).

Edgar Allan Poe read "The Raven" at the Lyceum in Boston on October 16, 1845. Most of the audience walked out before he finished reading.

October 17

Jean Craighead George used her experiences as a child living off the land with her father and brothers in the Potomac River wilderness to write *My Side of the Mountain* (1960 Newbery Honor Book).

At first, Ezra Jack Keats didn't intend for *The Snowy Day* (1963 Caldecott Medal) to be all collage. He simply wanted to use some special paper he had from Japan, Italy, Sweden, and the United States.

Only seven of William Shakespeare's autographs are known to exist. Each one is worth about $1,500,000.

October 18

Walter Edmonds didn't think he was writing for children when he wrote *The Matchlock Gun* (1942 Newbery Medal).

The 1973 Caldecott Honor Book, *Hosie's Alphabet*, became a family project after Leonard Baskin's three-year-old son asked him to draw an alphabet. Baskin gave family members Hosea, Tobias, and Lisa credit for their input.

When someone complained to Beatrix Potter that a word in *Benjamin Bunny* would be hard for children to understand, Potter suggested that children use a dictionary.

October 19

 BORN ON THIS DAY:
Ed Emberley, 1931

While reading Eleanor Estes's manuscript for *The Middle Moffat* (1943 Newbery Honor Book) on the subway, illustrator Louis Slobodkin laughed out loud. Other people on the train made sure they knew how to leave quickly just in case he *really* went crazy.

Ed Emberley thought *Drummer Hoff* (1968 Caldecott Medal) would have a small audience. He had no idea the book would become so popular.

The manuscript for *Little Toot* was rejected many times. Once the book was published, it became very popular. Walt Disney adapted the book into a cartoon and Little Toot appeared as a float in the Tournament of Roses Parade in Pasadena, California.

October 20

 BORN ON THIS DAY:
Atanas Katchamakoff, 1898

Monica Shannon based *Dobry* (1935 Newbery Medal) on many of the experiences of the book's illustrator, Atanas Katchamakoff.

Trina Schart Hyman's (*Little Red Riding Hood*, 1984 Caldecott Honor Book) mother made her a red cloak as a child. Her mother even called her "Red Riding Hood."

The Adventures of Tom Sawyer and *Adventures of Huckleberry Finn* are both on the list of 100 most influential books.

October 21

Meindert DeJong had two Newbery Honor Books in 1954: *Shadrach* and *Hurry Home, Candy*. The following year, his *The Wheel on the School* received the Newbery Medal.

Chris Van Allsburg (*Jumanji*, 1982 Caldecott Medal and *The Polar Express*, 1986 Caldecott Medal) and his classmates thought the Dewey Decimal System was fine, but they wanted to hear about the "Huey" and "Louie" systems as well.

Sir John Tenniel is most famous for illustrating Lewis Carroll's books about Alice, but he also illustrated for *Punch* magazine. Over the course of 30 years, his work appeared in all but two or three issues of the magazine.

October 22

Karen Hesse sent a manuscript about Bigfoot to editor Brenda Bowen, who liked Hesse's "Star Route" address, but rejected the manuscript. Several years later and at a different publishing company, Bowen again received an envelope with the "Star Route" address and remembered it. The manuscript inside became the book *Out of the Dust* (1998 Newbery Medal).

Stephen Gammell (*Song and Dance Man*, 1989 Caldecott Medal) asked for a manuscript rewrite with Grandpa doing more than singing and dancing. Author Karen Ackerman enthusiastically agreed to rewrite the story.

A teacher told a young Astrid Lindgren that she might become a writer when she grew up. Lindgren said she'd never be an author but grew up to write the Pippi Longstocking books.

October 23

Hendrik Van Loon (*The Story of Mankind*, 1922 Newbery Medal) was once seriously injured in a boat explosion.

Peggy Rathmann paid children $25.00 for each safety tip her editor accepted for the end papers in *Officer Buckle and Gloria* (1996 Caldecott Medal). Rathmann didn't realize how much the offer would cost her when she set the price.

The Betsy-Tacy books are based on the life of Maud Hart Lovelace, who grew up in Mankato, Minnesota. The background and incidents are mostly true, just "twisted about" to make the stories more interesting.

October 24

Shortly after she sent *Amos Fortune, Free Man* (1951 Newbery Medal) to her editor, Elizabeth Yates had a vivid dream of hitting the bullseye with an arrow. Her husband said the dream was easy to interpret, but he wouldn't tell his wife why until the book won the *Herald Tribune* Spring Festival Award.

From the time he was young, Gerald McDermott (*Arrow to the Sun*, 1975 Caldecott Medal) spent much of his time at the Detroit Institute of Arts.

When Hans Christian Andersen was a child, a fortune teller told his mother that he would have better luck than he deserved.

October 25

 BORN ON THIS DAY:
Carolyn Bailey, 1875

Carolyn Bailey's grandmother made the doll that became the basis for *Miss Hickory* (1947 Newbery Medal).

Doctors told Wanda Gág (*Millions of Cats*, 1929 Newbery Honor Book; *ABC Bunny*, 1934 Newbery Honor Book; *Snow White and the Seven Dwarfs*, 1939 Caldecott Honor Book, and *Nothing at All*, 1942 Caldecott Honor Book) that she had lung cancer and had three months to live. She lived for seventeen months and continued to work while she was in bed.

Dorothy Lathrop enjoyed the Bible story of Samson's foxes with the burning brands tied between their tails. She couldn't include the story in *Animals of the Bible* (1938 Caldecott Medal) for fear that a child might tie a burning brand to an animal's tail.

October 26

Jerry Spinelli based Amanda Beale's mother in *Maniac Magee* (1991 Newbery Medal) on a male dentist that Jerry's mother had gone to. Spinelli couldn't forget that dentist's kindness.

Paul Goble combined many legends to create *The Girl Who Loved Wild Horses* (1979 Caldecott Medal).

Children frequently give Sid Fleischman suggestions for new McBroom books, such as "McBroom goes to McDonald's."

October 27

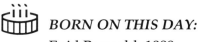 *BORN ON THIS DAY:*
Enid Bagnold, 1889

Although Mildred Taylor (*Roll of Thunder, Hear My Cry*, 1977 Newbery Medal) grew up in Ohio, she often traveled to the South.

John Schoenherr (*Owl Moon*, 1988 Caldecott Medal) spoke German until the age of three. When he couldn't make himself understood in the English-speaking community, he drew pictures to communicate.

Enid Bagnold's thirteen-year-old daughter, Laurian Jones, illustrated *National Velvet*, first published in 1930.

October 28

When Russell Freedman (*Lincoln: A Photobiography*, 1988 Newbery Medal) was a child, his teachers often sent him to the principal's office. He stared at a portrait of Lincoln while waiting outside the office.

The doll that inspired *Hitty: Her First Hundred Years* (1930 Newbery Medal) attended that year's Newbery Award ceremony.

Robert McCloskey bought four mallard ducks to use as models for *Make Way for Ducklings* (1942 Caldecott Medal). The ducks lived in the apartment bathtub.

October 29

Joan W. Blos said that winning the 1980 Newbery Medal for *A Gathering of Days* was like "going to the Rose Bowl and *winning*, and you hadn't even known that you were on the plane!"

A child once called Roger Duvoisin (*White Snow, Bright Snow*, 1948 Caldecott Medal) "the man who knows how to draw the weather."

L. Frank Baum chose the name for his magical kingdom in *The Wizard of Oz* when he saw a label on one of his file cabinet drawers that read "O-Z."

October 30

Elizabeth Janet Gray and Robert Lawson, author and illustrator of *Adam of the Road* (1943 Newbery Medal) were born ten years and two days apart.

Once he started writing *Fables* (1981 Caldecott Medal), Arnold Lobel wrote about one per day.

Mark Twain's father paid tuition of 25¢ per week for his son to attend school. When Twain was eleven, his father died. Twain worked to afford to attend school part-time, but soon dropped out completely.

October 31

 BORN ON THIS DAY:
Katherine Paterson, 1932

Katherine Paterson got the idea for *Bridge to Terabithia* (1978 Newbery Medal) after her son's best friend was killed by lightning.

James Marshall (*Goldilocks and the Three Bears*, 1989 Caldecott Medal) introduced himself to Maurice Sendak by sliding up to him on his knees and calling him "Master." The two became close friends.

Randolph Caldecott illustrated some of Washington Irving's works, including *Old Christmas: From the Sketchbook of Washington Irving* and *Bracebridge Hall*.

November 1

 BORN ON THIS DAY:
Stephen Crane, 1871

Lois Lowry hoped to be "charming and witty" on the *Today* show after winning the 1990 Newbery Medal for *Number the Stars*, but plane delays causing her to get less than four hours' sleep revised her hope to be "awake."

Berta and Elmer Hader used themselves as models for the man and woman in *The Big Snow* (1949 Caldecott Medal) because they fed the animals during a hard winter.

In *The Book of Literary Lists*, Stephen Crane's *The Red Badge of Courage* is named among the 100 most influential books.

November 2

The first book that James Daugherty illustrated was *Daniel Boone* (1940 Newbery Medal), written by Stuart Edward White. Daniel Boone was born on this day in 1734.

The largest "book store" Peter Sis (*Starry Messenger*, 1997 Caldecott Honor Book and *Tibet: Through The Red Box*, 1999 Caldecott Honor Book) remembers from childhood is the library in his own home.

At age seventeen, Hans Christian Andersen enrolled in grammar school with eleven-year-old classmates.

November 3

Beverly Cleary (*Dear Mr. Henshaw*, 1984 Newbery Medal) used the name Henshaw after seeing it in an obituary column.

Elizabeth Enright (*Thimble Summer*, 1939 Newbery Medal) served as a model for Heidi while her mother, Maginel Wright Enright, illustrated the book about the mountain girl.

A drawing of a geisha by Paul Zelinsky (*Rapunzel*, 1998 Caldecott Medal) appeared in the November 1957 *Highlights* magazine. He was three years old at the time.

November 4

 BORN ON THIS DAY:
Gail Haley, 1939

As a child, Doris Gates (*Blue Willow*, 1941 Newbery Honor Book) once received a burro for Christmas.

Gail Haley spent a year researching *A Story, A Story* (1971 Caldecott Medal) including learning African dancing and cooking. She spent another year working on the book.

Pinocchio author Carlo Collodi dropped out of seminary school at age sixteen.

November 5

Cynthia Voigt (*Dicey's Song*, 1983 Newbery Medal) said that because she won the Newbery Medal, she had to learn the correct spelling of it—only one "r."

In his acceptance speech for *Make Way for Ducklings* (1942 Caldecott Medal), Robert McCloskey said he wished he could draw pictures or play the harmonica instead of make a speech.

Since publication in 1936, Ernest Hemingway's short story "The Snows of Kilimanjaro" has earned more than $500,000 in movie and reprint rights.

November 6

The Story of Mankind (1922 Newbery Medal) was the second-best-selling nonfiction book in 1922 and the ninth-best-selling nonfiction book in 1923.

David Wiesner (*Tuesday*, 1992 Caldecott Medal) became interested in wordless storytelling after seeing *Mad Man's Drums* by Lynd Ward (*The Biggest Bear*, 1953 Caldecott Medal).

Rudyard Kipling was the first English author to win the Nobel prize.

November 7

 BORN ON THIS DAY:
Armstrong Sperry, 1897

As a child, Armstrong Sperry (*Call It Courage*, 1941 Newbery Medal) read books on the South Seas that made him "long to throw all my schoolbooks out the window and stow away on the first ship I could find that was sailing south."

Muriel Feelings wrote *Moja Means One: Swahili Counting Book* (1972 Caldecott Honor Book) while informally teaching Swahili to interested students during the time she taught regular classes in Brooklyn, New York.

As a boy, Thornton W. Burgess wanted to be a naturalist, but his mother wanted him to be a preacher. Burgess said he achieved both through his writing, only he preached about nature instead of the Bible.

November 8

Katherine Paterson was worried her secular publisher would reject *The Great Gilly Hopkins* (1979 Newbery Honor Book) because the basic story is that of the Prodigal Son. Conversely, a group of parents tried to get the book banned in their school district for having an "anti-Christian" message.

For *The Snowy Day* (1963 Caldecott Medal), Ezra Jack Keats used a toothbrush to splatter India ink to create the background on the pages where Peter goes to sleep.

As an adult, Eric Carle has only minimal interest in reading children's books, even though he writes and illustrates for children.

November 9

 BORN ON THIS DAY:
Lois Ehlert, 1934

In her acceptance speech for *The Grey King* (1976 Newbery Medal), Susan Cooper said that giving the Newbery to a "Limey" in the bicentennial year shows the "rugged independence of the Children's Services Division [of the American Library Association]."

Lois Ehlert's (*Color Zoo*, 1990 Caldecott Honor Book) first drawing board was a bread board propped up against a can on a card table.

Johann Wyss wrote the manuscript for *Swiss Family Robinson* but didn't submit it to publishers. Many years after he wrote it, Wyss's son found the manuscript and submitted it to a publisher.

November 10

 BORN ON THIS DAY:
Kate Seredy, 1889

Kate Seredy spent only three weeks writing *The White Stag* (1938 Newbery Medal).

Leo Lionni's first career was as an artist and graphic designer. He didn't start writing and illustrating children's books, including his four Caldecott Honor Books, until he was a grandfather telling stories to his grandchildren.

At a picnic, J. M. Barrie overheard a mother telling her son that he would become sick if he ate more chocolates. The boy said, "I shall be sick tonight," and continued eating. Barrie paid the boy a halfpenny a performance of *Peter Pan* for using that line.

November 11

Because his father's job caused his family to frequently relocate, William Pène du Bois (*The Twenty-One Balloons*, 1948 Newbery Medal) didn't do well in his school writing classes. He always seemed to be speaking English when he was in France and speaking French when he was in the United States.

Maud and Miska Petersham (*The Rooster Crows*, 1946 Caldecott Medal) joked about needing each other to produce a book because she was left-handed and he was right-handed.

Some of the pseudonyms Samuel Langhorne Clemens used, besides Mark Twain, were Carl Byng, G. Ragsdale McClintock, and Thomas Jefferson Snodgrass.

November 12

The father of Elizabeth Borton de Treviño (*I, Juan de Pareja*, 1966 Newbery Medal) rented a small office and paid his daughter a salary to encourage her to keep regular office hours for her writing.

Being hit by a car sent Ludwig Bemelmans to the hospital. The title character in *Madeline*

(1940 Caldecott Honor Book) had her appendix removed because a girl across the hall from Bemelmans in the hospital had *her* appendix removed.

Dr. Seuss wrote *The Cat in the Hat* in response to an article objecting to supplementary readers used in schools.

November 13

 BORN ON THIS DAY:
Robert Louis Stevenson, 1850

A banner decorating the room during the awards ceremony for *The Summer of the Swans* (1971 Newbery Medal) contained genuine swan feathers that were hand sewn to the material.

During the illustration process of *Always Room for One More* (1966 Caldecott Medal), Sorche Nic Leodhas told Nonny Hogrogian that her first effort at drawing a Scotsman gave him more of the bone structure of a Romanian than a Scotsman.

From the time he was a child, ill health often confined Robert Louis Stevenson to bed. His poor health didn't prevent him from traveling throughout the world, though.

November 14

 BORN ON THIS DAY:
Miska Miles, 1899
William Steig, 1907

Miska Miles, pen name of Patricia Miles Martin, grew up reading everything she could find about Native American culture. *Annie and the Old One* (1972 Newbery Honor Book) grew out of that interest.

According to William Steig's son, *Sylvester and the Magic Pebble* (1970 Caldecott Medal) is about love.

Moby Dick was first published on November 14, 1851.

November 15

 BORN ON THIS DAY:
Daniel Pinkwater, 1941

Irene Hunt (*Up a Road Slowly*, 1967 Newbery Medal) worked at her kitchen table. She had a desk in the den but felt it was "much too proper" to write comfortably there.

Leo Dillon and Diane Dillon (*Why Mosquitoes Buzz in People's Ears*, 1976 Caldecott Medal and *Ashanti to Zulu*, 1977 Caldecott Medal) were two of the best students that Parsons School ever had.

In elections, Daniel Pinkwater votes for fictional characters.

November 16

 BORN ON THIS DAY:
Robin McKinley, 1952

Robin McKinley compared Aerin's battle with the dragon in *The Hero and the Crown* (1985 Newbery Medal) to living in an urban slum. At the time she wrote the book, McKinley lived in a run-down section of Staten Island, New York.

Audrey Wood (*King Bidgood's in the Bathtub*, 1986 Caldecott Honor Book) spent part of her childhood near the winter quarters of the Ringling Brothers Circus and part of her childhood traveling with a band of gypsies.

S. E. Hinton said reading taught her many things, except "strangely enough" it didn't teach her how to spell.

November 17

Karen Cushman (*The Midwife's Apprentice*, 1996 Newbery Medal) refused to learn how to type to avoid having to make her living as a secretary.

The first attempts Evaline Ness (*Sam, Bangs and Moonshine*, 1967 Caldecott Medal) made at art consisted of cutting pictures from magazines to illustrate the stories her older sister wrote.

Crowds waited at a New York pier for the ship carrying the magazine with an installment of Charles Dickens's *Old Curiosity Shop*. Even before the ship docked, people shouted, "Is Little Nell dead?" to the people on the ship.

November 18

E. L. Konigsburg (*From the Mixed-up Files of Mrs. Basil E. Frankweiler*, 1968 Newbery Medal and *The View from Saturday*, 1997 Newbery Medal) found that going from being a chemist to being a writer was easier than going from being a smoker to being a nonsmoker.

While working on *Swamp Angel* (1995 Caldecott Honor Book), Paul Zelinsky made a Swamp Angel from bent wire wrapped in paper tape.

Judith Viorst's first published books were nonfiction science books.

November 19

BORN ON THIS DAY:
Margaret Musgrove, 1943
Jack Schaefer, 1907

Jack Schaefer's book *Old Ramon* was a 1961 Newbery Honor Book, but Schaefer is best known for writing the western *Shane*.

E. B. White (*Charlotte's Web*, 1953 Newbery Honor Book) said, "A book is a sneeze."

Margaret Musgrove, author of *Ashanti to Zulu* (1997 Caldecott Medal) lived and traveled in West Africa while she was an English teacher in Ghana.

November 20

Katherine Paterson quoted Paul Simon and Art Garfunkel's song "Bridge Over Troubled Water" in her acceptance speech for *Bridge to Terabithia* (1978 Newbery Medal).

Lane Smith and Jon Scieszka (*The Stinky Cheese Man and Other Fairly Stupid Tales*, 1993 Caldecott Honor Book) cite the same influences: Monty Python, *Mad* magazine, and comic books.

Randolph Caldecott often visited Walter Crane's home where he frequently played with the Crane children.

Lewis Carroll based the Alice in his books on Alice Liddell, the daughter of the dean at Christ Church, but according to *The Annotated Alice* by Martin Gardner, John Tenniel may have used Mary Hilton Badcock, another of Carroll's young friends, as a model for the illustrations.

November 21

BORN ON THIS DAY:
Leo Politi, 1908
Elizabeth George Speare, 1908

Elizabeth George Speare (*The Witch of Blackbird Pond*, 1959 Newbery Medal and *The Bronze Bow*, 1962 Newbery Medal) wrote stories as a child but didn't begin writing seriously until her children were in junior high school.

In 1955, Alice Dalgliesh's book *The Courage of Sarah Noble* was a Newbery Honor Book and her book *The Thanksgiving Story* was a Caldecott Honor Book.

Leo Politi (*Song of the Swallows*, 1950 Caldecott Medal) enjoyed drawing children more than any other subject. He tried to depict warmth and happiness of family life; love for people, animals, birds, and flowers; and love of simple, warm, and earthy things.

Leo Politi and Elizabeth George Speare were born on the same day on opposite coasts (Politi in California and Speare in Massachusetts).

November 22

Paul Fleischman's enjoyment of creating music with others played a large role in his writing process for *Joyful Noise* (1989 Newbery Medal).

After reading *Ox-Cart Man* (1980 Caldecott Medal), Cynthia Rylant (*When I Was Young in the Mountains*, 1983 Caldecott Honor Book; *The Relatives Came*, 1986 Caldecott Honor Book; *A Fine White Dust*, 1987 Newbery Honor Book; and *Missing May*, 1993 Newbery Medal) started writing from the heart instead of what she called "stupid little fantasy stories."

In France, Curious George is known as Fifi.

November 23

BORN ON THIS DAY:
Marc Simont, 1915

Zilpha Keatley Snyder wanted *The Egypt Game* (1968 Newbery Honor Book) to be a fantasy, but she said the story was "too head-strong" to be one.

Marc Simont's (*A Tree Is Nice*, 1957 Caldecott Medal) father, two uncles, and sister are all artists. Simont learned to write, in addition to illustrate, while he recuperated from chicken pox.

The first time Beatrix Potter wrote about Flopsy, Mopsy, Cottontail, and Peter in Mr. McGregor's garden was in a letter to a sick boy named Noel, the son of a former governess. Noel saved the letter and eight years later Potter used the story as the basis of a book.

November 24

BORN ON THIS DAY:
Frances Hodgson Burnett, 1849
Carlo Collodi, 1826

When Lloyd Alexander finished writing *The High King* (1969 Newbery Medal), he felt as if "something [he] had loved deeply for a long time had suddenly gone away."

John Steptoe (*The Story of Jumping Mouse*, 1985 Caldecott Honor Book and *Mufaro's Beautiful Daughters*, 1988 Caldecott Honor Book) wrote with the intention of including genuine African American dialogue because he saw so few books that reflected the speech of African American children.

Frances Hodgson Burnett, author of *A Little Princess*, *Little Lord Fauntleroy*, and *The Secret Garden*, didn't receive even one rejection in her writing career.

Pinocchio creator Carlo Collodi's real name was Carlo Lorenzini. He took his pen name from Castello Collodi in Valdineme, Italy.

November 25

BORN ON THIS DAY:
Marc Brown, 1946

According to a 1976 *Publishers Weekly* survey, *Johnny Tremain* (1944 Newbery Medal) is considered the seventh best children's book written in America.

Maurice Sendak (*Where the Wild Things Are*, 1964 Caldecott Medal) thought that the talents of Richard Egielski and Arthur Yorinks (illustrator and author of *Hey, Al!*, 1987 Caldecott Medal) would complement each other, so he arranged a meeting between them.

Marc Brown based his character Arthur on a combination of himself and his two sons.

November 26

As a child, William H. Armstrong (*Sounder*, 1970 Newbery Medal) enjoyed the Bible because he could use his imagination to fill in the spaces left by the limited descriptions.

Peter Sis (*Starry Messenger*, 1997 Caldecott Honor Book and *Tibet: Through the Red Box*, 1999 Caldecott Honor Book) worked as a disc jockey while he attended art school.

Two versions of *Puss In Boots* were named Caldecott Honor Books. One was illustrated by Marcia Brown (1953), and the other was illustrated by Fred Marcellino (1991).

November 27

 BORN ON THIS DAY:

Kevin Henkes, 1960

Katherine Milhous, 1894

While writing her first book, Elizabeth Enright (*Thimble Summer*, 1939 Newbery Medal) learned she liked writing more than illustrating, and from then on she didn't illustrate anyone else's books.

Lois Lowry once interviewed painter Carl Nelson who later became blind. She thought about how he must have felt when he lost the ability to see the colors that had been his life. Her thoughts inspired *The Giver* (1994 Newbery Medal). The face on the cover of the book is that of Carl Nelson.

For Easter, the Historical Society of Reading, Pennsylvania exhibited a tree decorated with 1,400 eggs. It inspired Katherine Milhous to create *The Egg Tree* (1951 Caldecott Medal).

Kevin Henkes (*Owen*, 1994 Caldecott Medal) considers himself lucky because ever since childhood he wanted to be an artist and a writer, and he now makes his living illustrating and writing.

November 28

 BORN ON THIS DAY:

Ed Young, 1931

Karen Hesse once mistakenly watered one of her husband's plants with vinegar. The plant died. Similarly, in Hesse's *Out of the Dust* (1998 Newbery Medal), the mother grabs the wrong pail and pours kerosene on a fire.

In 1953, Ed Young (*Lon Po Po*, 1990 Caldecott Medal) won a contest to design a badge for the homecoming football game at the University of Illinois, where he was studying architecture. Winning gave him the courage to pursue his career as a artist.

Robert McCloskey said he would have done the illustrations for *Make Way for Ducklings* (1942 Caldecott Medal) in color if he would have known the technique of color separation at the time.

A scene in John Newbery's *Goody Two-Shoes* describes the death of the main character's father when he was "seized with a violent fever in a place where Dr James'[s] Powder was not to be had." Dr James's Powder was an actual medicine that Newbery produced and sold.

November 29

 BORN ON THIS DAY:

Louisa May Alcott, 1832

Madeline L'Engle, 1918

C. S. Lewis, 1898

Madeline L'Engle's *A Wrinkle in Time* (1963 Newbery Medal) is credited with being a major turning point in juvenile science fiction, while at the same time it is condemned for being similar to George Orwell's *1984*.

Before beginning work on *Noah's Ark* (1978 Caldecott Medal), Peter Spier investigated how many other books about Noah were available. In examining the more than twenty books he found, Spier saw that most either showed no imagination or showed the flood as a "joyous, sun-filled Caribbean cruise." Spier knew he could do better—such as show Noah battling flies and shoveling manure.

Louisa May Alcott was born on her father's thirty-third birthday. She and her father died two days apart on March 4 and March 6, 1888.

C. S. Lewis signed some of his poems "N. W." or "Nat Whilk," which is an Anglo Saxon term for "I know not who."

November 30

 BORN ON THIS DAY:

Lucy Maud Montgomery, 1874
Jonathan Swift, 1667
Mark Twain, 1835
Margot Zemach, 1931

Marguerite de Angeli based the character of Robin in *The Door in the Wall* (1950 Newbery Medal) on a disabled friend who became a violinist, as well as a cabinet maker and a crafts artist.

Margot Zemach (*Duffy and the Devil*, 1974 Caldecott Medal) often worked with one cat on her lap and another cat drinking the paint water.

Lucy Maud Montgomery started to submit her writing when she was eleven years old. She sold her first poem at age fifteen. *Anne of Green Gables*, her first book, was published when she was thirty-four years old.

Jonathan Swift first published *Gulliver's Travels* anonymously in 1726 as *Travels into Several Remote Nations of the World* in four parts by Lemuel Gulliver.

Halley's Comet appeared the year Mark Twain was born and didn't appear again until the year Twain died.

December 1

Carolyn Bailey based Mr. T. Willard-Brown in *Miss Hickory* (1947 Newbery Medal) on one of the twenty-three barn cats she owned. She chose Tippy because he had a scar on his nose from a fight with a rat. Bailey changed the cat's name because "Tippy" didn't sound dignified enough.

Pedro, The Angel of Olvera Street (1947 Caldecott Honor Book) began as a Christmas card that Leo Politi sent to his editor who asked him to write and illustrate a book about Christmas on Olvera Street.

In 1952 Frederic Melcher visited the office of editor Margaret McElderry to tell her that the Harper book *Finders Keepers* had won the Caldecott Award and the Harper book *Ginger Pye* had won the Newbery Award.

December 2

 BORN ON THIS DAY:
David Macaulay, 1946

As a child, Mari Sandoz (*The Horsecatcher*, 1958 Newbery Honor Book) had to sneak books into her house because her father disapproved of reading fiction.

David Macaulay (*Black and White*, 1991 Caldecott Medal) intended to become an architect. He didn't think of becoming an illustrator even though, as a teenager, he copied every picture of the Beatles that he could find.

On December 2, 1867, people in New York City stood in two lines almost a mile long for tickets to see Charles Dickens reading from his works for the first time in America.

December 3

A month before *The Hero and the Crown* (1985 Newbery Medal) was due at the publishers, author Robin McKinley broke her ankle. Shortly before the deadline for *The Blue Sword* (1983 Newbery Honor Book), McKinley broke her hand when a horse fell on her.

The last item Leo Dillon and Diane Dillon had to find for their research for *Ashanti to Zulu* (1977 Caldecott Medal) was a picture of the Lozi barge.

Esphyr Slobodkina, author/illustrator of *Caps for Sale* and other books, grew up in a small Siberian town. Many peddlers carrying their wares with them passed through the area.

December 4

 BORN ON THIS DAY:
Munro Leaf, 1905

Hendrik Van Loon (*The Story of Mankind*, 1922 Newbery Medal) was working on a book about his childhood at the time of his death. Ironically, his working title for the book was *Report to St. Peter*.

Elizabeth Orton Jones searched long and hard for just the right toys to use as models for *Prayer for a Child* (1945 Caldecott Medal). In addition to being the right size and shape, the toys had to be worn enough to show they were loved, yet not so worn they'd lost their shape.

Munro Leaf wrote *The Story of Ferdinand* on a yellow legal pad in less than an hour for his friend Robert Lawson to illustrate.

December 5

BORN ON THIS DAY:
Ann Nolan Clark, 1896
Harve Zemach, 1933

Ann Nolan Clark (*Secret of the Andes*, 1953 Newbery Medal) wrote with the intention of producing books *for*, not *about* Native Americans.

Harvey Fishchtrom (*Duffy and the Devil*, 1974 Caldecott Medal) used the name Harve Zemach when working with his wife, Margot Zemach.

In a December 1891 letter to Alice Liddell Hargreaves, the married name of the girl on which he based the Alice in his books, Lewis Carroll wrote that "her" adventures had sold more than 100,000 copies.

December 6

BORN ON THIS DAY:
Cornelia Meigs, 1884
Elizabeth Yates, 1905

As a child, Elizabeth Yates (*Amos Fortune, Free Man*, 1951 Newbery Medal) tried copying the letters in the books she read, but her nurse scolded her for "scribbling" on the pages.

While growing up, Cornelia Meigs (*Invincible Louisa*, 1934 Newbery Medal) read and re-read *Louisa Alcott's Life Letters and Journals*.

Rachel Isadora (*Ben's Trumpet*, 1980 Caldecott Honor Book) was a professional dancer by age eleven. After a foot injury forced her to retire from ballet dancing before she was thirty, she turned to writing and illustrating.

Jules Verne, author of *Twenty Thousand Leagues Under the Sea* and other books, predicted inventions such as the incandescent light bulb, radio, electric clock, submarine, and other items.

December 7

Paul Fleischman wanted to do a sequel to his *I Am Phoenix*, but thought sequels were for "Nancy Drew and Rocky." He did eventually write the sequel *Joyful Noise* (1989 Newbery Medal) after many false starts.

They Were Strong and Good (1941 Caldecott Medal) has been criticized for portraying slaves cheerfully going about their duties and crying when their master goes off to war.

Mark Twain was the first person to submit a manuscript (*The Adventures of Tom Sawyer*, first published in 1876) on typewritten pages. He kept the information secret because he didn't want to give instructions on how to use typewriters or to give testimonials for typewriters.

December 8

BORN ON THIS DAY:
James Thurber, 1894

Beverly Cleary (*Dear Mr. Henshaw*, 1984 Newbery Medal) learned a lot about trucks from her son who worked with many truckers.

James Thurber (*Many Moons*, 1944 Caldecott Medal) lost the vision in one eye in a childhood accident. He was completely blind the last years of his life but wrote by dictating into a tape recorder.

William Shakespeare chose to sit in the corner of the classroom so other students wouldn't distract him from his studies.

December 9

BORN ON THIS DAY:

Joan W. Blos, 1928

Jean de Brunhoff, 1899

Joel Chandler Harris, 1899

The idea for *A Gathering of Days* (1980 Newbery Medal) developed from Joan W. Blos's fascination with her husband's house in New Hampshire. Many of the events in the book are based on actual occurrences she found during her twelve years of research.

The first time Verna Aardema (*Why Mosquitoes Buzz in People's Ears*, 1976 Caldecott Medal) remembered being noticed for a *good* reason was for getting an "A" on a poem she'd written.

Stories that Jean de Brunhoff's wife told her children about a little elephant became the basis for the books about Babar.

Joel Chandler Harris, author of the Uncle Remus stories, was so shy he couldn't speak before groups and even stammered when speaking to his own children.

December 10

BORN ON THIS DAY:

Emily Dickinson, 1830

Sid Fleischman kept giving up on the manuscript for *The Whipping Boy* (1987 Newbery Medal) because he couldn't get it "right."

William Steig said his acceptance speech for *Sylvester and the Magic Pebble* (1970 Caldecott Medal) shouldn't be as long as the book. The book has approximately 1,400 words, and his speech had close to 650 words.

Emily Dickinson didn't leave her home at all during the last 20 years of her life.

December 11

Under doctor's orders, Robert C. O'Brien couldn't deliver his own acceptance speech for *Mrs. Frisby and the Rats of NIMH* (1972 Newbery Medal). His editor read the speech for him.

Thanks to the Transatlantic telephone, 500 people in Paris listened to Roger Duvoisin's acceptance speech for the 1948 Caldecott Medal, which he received for *White Snow, Bright Snow*.

Eric Knight, author of *Lassie Come Home*, owned a collie originally named Lassie, but he later changed the dog's name to Toots.

December 12

BORN ON THIS DAY:

Barbara Emberley, 1932

Dorothy Lathrop had a difficult time illustrating *Hitty: Her First Hundred Years* (1930 Newbery Medal) because she couldn't use varied facial expressions on the doll, only body and limb positions.

Barbara Emberley (*Drummer Hoff*, 1968 Caldecott Medal) writes the books that she and her husband, Ed, create. She and Ed share "the thousand and one things that turn pictures into books" including research, preparation of art for the printer, typeface and ink selection, and more—everything but the actual drawing, which is done solely by Ed.

George Orwell once absentmindedly ate the boiled eels meant for the cat instead of the shepherd's pie his wife had left for him.

December 13

 BORN ON THIS DAY:
Leonard Weisgard, 1916

The House of Sixty Fathers (1957 Newbery Honor Book) is based on author Meindert DeJong's wartime experience in occupied China.

Leonard Weisgard used Vinalhaven, an island off the coast of Maine, as a model for the illustrations in *The Little Island* (1947 Caldecott Medal).

The Dr. Seuss books have sold more than 200 million copies and have been translated into more than twenty languages, including Braille.

December 14

Sharon Creech wrote two versions of *Walk Two Moons* (1995 Newbery Medal) before the final published version. Salmanaca wasn't in either draft.

While writing *Madeline* (1940 Caldecott Honor Book), Ludwig Bemelmans used some of his mother's memories of her childhood in a convent in Bavaria.

H. A. Rey's first recognizable drawing, done at age two, wasn't of a monkey like Curious George, but of a man on a horse.

December 15

Arthur B. Chrisman kept his 1926 Newbery Medal for *Shen of the Sea* in a safety deposit box with three shares of Montana copper stock "and not much else."

Paul Zelinsky wasn't expecting the call he received from the Caldecott Committee telling him he had won the 1998 Caldecott Medal for *Rapunzel* because it was Monday and they had called him on a Tuesday to tell him that *Swamp Angel* was a 1995 Caldecott Honor Book.

Daniel Pinkwater owns what could be the largest and most complete set of false noses in the world.

December 16

 BORN ON THIS DAY:
Marie Hall Ets, 1895
Nicolas Sidjakov, 1924

Russell Freedman's (*Lincoln: A Photobiography*, 1988 Newbery Medal) parents met in a San Francisco book store. His mother was a clerk there, and his father was a publisher's representative.

Marie Hall Ets (*Nine Days to Christmas*, 1960 Caldecott Medal) was born nine days before Christmas.

Nicolas Sidjakov (*Babushka and the Three Kings*, 1961 Caldecott Medal) designed the poster for Orson Welles's film *Othello*.

December 17

 BORN ON THIS DAY:
David Kherdian, 1931
William Lipkind, 1904

David Kherdian didn't know whether to send the manuscript for *The Road from Home* (1980 Newbery Honor Book) to a publisher for adults or a publisher for children. He decided to try a children's publisher first and received an acceptance.

William Lipkind attended Columbia Law School. His law experience may have played a part in the plot of *Finders Keepers* (1952 Caldecott Medal).

Edgar Allan Poe long-jumped twenty-one feet while he attended West Point.

December 18

Paula Fox saw a footnote about slave ship crews often kidnapping young street musicians to play music on board ship so that the slaves would dance and, therefore, exercise. That single footnote sparked the idea for *The Slave Dancer* (1974 Newbery Medal).

A little girl who met Maud and Miska Petersham (*The Rooster Crows*, 1946 Caldecott Medal) was disappointed to see they were real people because she had thought they were magic.

Editor May Massee once thought Robert Lawson would be the perfect illustrator for a project but was sure he had died. When she saw one of his drawings in a magazine, she realized he was alive and called him. They worked together many years, producing two Caldecott Medal books, one Newbery Medal book, a Caldecott Honor Book, and a Newbery Honor Book.

December 19

 *BORN ON THIS DAY:*
Eve Bunting, 1928
Eleanor H. Porter, 1868

E. B. White did nine drafts of *Charlotte's Web* (1953 Newbery Honor Book).

Although *Smoky Night* (1995 Caldecott Medal) is set in California, many of Eve

Bunting's other books incorporate her own Irish background.

Eleanor H. Porter's *Pollyanna* was eighth on the fiction best-seller list in 1913, and it was second in 1914.

December 20

 BORN ON THIS DAY:
Richard Atwater, 1892

Many publishers rejected Richard Atwater's manuscript for *Mr. Popper's Penguins* (1939 Newbery Honor Book) until his wife, Florence, revised the manuscript.

Virginia Hamilton (*M. C. Higgins the Great*, 1975 Newbery Medal) once had three goals: to visit New York, to visit Spain, and to be a writer. She achieved all three.

Maurice Sendak (*Where the Wild Things Are*, 1964 Caldecott Medal) and Arthur Yorinks (*Hey, Al!*, 1987 Caldecott Medal) founded a children's theater called In the Night Kitchen.

December 21

 BORN ON THIS DAY:
Feodor Rojankovsky, 1891

When the Library of Congress asked Jean Lee Latham for permission to record *Carry On, Mr. Bowditch* (1956 Newbery Medal) for Talking Books for the Blind, Latham asked if she could be the reader because she was once a drama student. She auditioned and got the job.

When Susan Cooper saw nearly 2,000 people in the room where she had to give her acceptance speech for the 1976 Newbery Medal for her book *The Grey King*, she whispered to her editor, "I don't believe I ever want to win the Newbery."

Feodor Rojankovsky (*Frog Went A-Courtin'*, 1956 Caldecott Medal) sent his editor Margaret McElderry many letters decorated with frogs.

December 22

 BORN ON THIS DAY:
Jerry Pinkney, 1939

Walter Edmonds wrote most of *The Matchlock Gun* (1942 Newbery Medal) in two days.

As a hobby, Gary Paulsen runs dogsleds and has participated in the Iditarod. His book *Dogsong* (1986 Newbery Honor Book) is based on those experiences.

Jerry Pinkney once worked at a newspaper stand where he spent his free time sketching store display windows and people he saw. A passing cartoonist suggested he try to earn a living with his art. Pinkney went on to illustrate three Caldecott Honor Books: *Mirandy and Brother Wind* (1989), *The Talking Eggs* (1990), and *John Henry* (1995).

December 23

 BORN ON THIS DAY:
Avi, 1937

A television producer offered to buy the rights to *The True Confessions of Charlotte Doyle* (1991 Newbery Honor Book). Author Avi declined because the deal would have included drastically changing the ending.

Sid Fleischman gave Jemmy a sister at the request of TV producers who wanted him to add a strong female character for the screen version of *The Whipping Boy* (1987 Newbery Medal).

David Weisner studied nature photographs and sculpted a frog model in clay to help him make the illustrations for *Tuesday* (1992 Caldecott Medal) appear more real.

December 24

 BORN ON THIS DAY:
John Langstaff, 1920
Noel Streatfield, 1895

Robin McKinley (*The Hero and the Crown*, 1985 Newbery Medal) said her epitaph should read, "There must have been an easier way."

John Langstaff (*Frog Went A-Courtin'*, 1956 Caldecott Medal) sang publicly from the time he was a child. Musician Bob Dylan recorded the song "Froggie Went A-Courtin'" on his 1992 album *Good As I Been to You*.

Clement C. Moore first recited "A Visit from St. Nicholas" for his ailing daughter at an 1822 Christmas Eve celebration.

Noel Streatfield, author of *Ballet Shoes*, was a professional actress specializing in Shakespearean plays.

December 25

 BORN ON THIS DAY:
Charles Finger, 1869

At various times, Charles Finger (*Tales From Silver Lands*, 1925 Newbery Medal) worked as a gold prospector in the Klondike, a sailor, a guide on ornithological exhibitions, a boilermaker's helper, a director of a music conservatory, and more.

Chris Van Allsburg once saw the image of a train standing still in front of his house which gave him the idea for *The Polar Express* (1986 Caldecott Medal).

On his son's first birthday, A. A. Milne gave him a toy bear purchased at Harrod's in London. Milne's son, Christopher Robin, named the bear Winnie-the-Pooh.

December 26

Lois Lowry based *Number the Stars* (1990 Newbery Medal) on a friend's childhood memories of Copenhagen.

The only others allowed in Louis Sachar's (*Holes*, 1999 Newbery Medal) work area while he's writing are his dogs.

The first time Robert McCloskey (*Make Way for Ducklings*, 1942 Caldecott Medal) met his editor May Massee, they went to dinner. McCloskey ordered duck.

In 1928, Lewis Carroll's original manuscript of *Alice's Adventures in Wonderland* sold for 15,400 British pounds.

December 27

 BORN ON THIS DAY:

Ingri d'Aulaire, 1904

Dhan Mukerji worked on the manuscript for *Gay-Neck: The Story of a Pigeon* (1928 Newbery Medal) in the mornings. In the afternoons, he sat on the beach near his home and read what he had written to area children.

Ingri and Parin d'Aulaire spent several weeks on a camping trip while they gathered information for *Abraham Lincoln* (1940 Caldecott Medal).

Peter Pan opened at the Duke of York's Theatre in London on December 27, 1904.

December 28

 BORN ON THIS DAY:

Carol Ryrie Brink, 1895

Emily Neville, 1919

In addition to writing such books as *Caddie Woodlawn* (1936 Newbery Medal), Carol Ryrie Brink also wrote poetry and several successful plays.

It's Like This, Cat (1964 Newbery Medal) began as a short story called "Cat and I." Expanding the story into a book took two years, in part because author Emily Neville had to turn the ribbon of her malfunctioning typewriter by hand every few words.

Three versions of Mother Goose rhymes are Caldecott Honor Books: *Mother Goose* by Tasha Tudor (1945), *Book of Nursery and Mother Goose Rhymes* by Marguerite de Angeli (1955), and *Mother Goose and Nursery Rhymes* by Philip Reed (1964).

December 29

 BORN ON THIS DAY:

Molly Bang, 1943

Kate Seredy (*The White Stag*, 1938 Newbery Medal) came to the United States for a short visit in 1922. In 1955 she said she was like "The Man Who Came to Dinner" because she was still in America.

Meindert DeJong was born with a caul (a membrane covering her face). The superstition at the time said that a baby born with a caul would have great adversity at the beginning of his life and fame later in life. Before he was even old enough to enroll in school, he suffered through three serious bouts of pneumonia. Later in life, he won the 1955 Newbery Medal for *The Wheel on the School*, as well as four Newbery Honor Awards (*Hurry Home Candy*, 1954; *Shadrach*, 1954; *House of Sixty Fathers*, 1957; *Along Came a Dog*, 1959).

Molly Bang's parents were both involved in medical research. Molly illustrated health manuals in Calcutta and Bangladesh for UNICEF and Johns Hopkins Center for Medical Research and Training before going on to write and illustrate books including the Caldecott Honor Books *The Grey Lady and the Strawberry Snatcher* (1981) and *Ten, Nine, Eight* (1984).

December 30

 BORN ON THIS DAY:
Rudyard Kipling, 1865
Mercer Mayer, 1943

During his Newbery Medal acceptance speech, Jerry Spinelli (*Maniac Magee*, 1991 Newbery Medal) thanked his editor for taking a chance on publishing a book about a hero who has no home or family and doesn't attend school.

Donald Hall (*Ox-Cart Man*, 1980 Caldecott Medal) first wrote a poem about the ox-cart man which was published in *The New Yorker*. Later, he decided the story would make a good book for children.

Mercer Mayer says he creates stories using mostly pictures and sometimes a few words. He doesn't like to tell stories aloud because he thinks he lacks verbal skills.

Rudyard Kipling was named for Rudyard Lake, Staffordshire, where his parents first met.

December 31

Katherine Paterson said that children in Sunday School are only taught "A friend loveth at all times," but never the rest of Proverbs 17:17, which reads "but a brother is born for adversity." She used that concept in *Jacob Have I Loved* (1981 Newbery Medal).

Some art instructors told Leo Dillon (*Why Mosquitoes Buzz in People's Ears*, 1976 Caldecott Medal and *Ashanti to Zulu*, 1977 Caldecott Medal) that he would never be successful because he is African American.

The gold Newbery and Caldecott Medals given to the winning author and illustrator are actually made of bronze.

THE NEWBERY MEDAL WINNERS

Because several editions exist for many of these books, only the original illustrators and publishers are listed. Where no illustrator is listed, none exists.

1922—*The Story of Mankind.* Written and illustrated by Hendrik Willem Van Loon. (Liveright)

Honor Books:

- *The Great Quest.* Written by Charles Hawes. Illustrated by George Varian. (Little, Brown)
- *Cedric the Forester.* Written and illustrated by Bernard Marshall. (Appleton-Century)
- *The Old Tobacco Shop.* Written and illustrated by William Bowen. (Macmillan)
- *The Golden Fleece and the Heroes Who Lived Before Achilles.* Written by Padraic Colum. Illustrated by Willy Pogany. (Macmillan)
- *The Windy Hill.* Written by Cornelia Meigs. (Macmillan)

1923—*The Voyages of Doctor Dolittle.* Written and illustrated by Hugh Lofting. (Lippincott)

Honor Books:

- No Record

1924—*The Dark Frigate.* Written by Charles Boardman Hawes. Illustrated by Anton Otto Fischer. (Little, Brown)

Honor Books:

- No Record

1925—*Tales from Silver Lands.* Written by Charles J. Finger. Illustrated by Paul Honoré. (Doubleday)

Honor Books:

- *Nicholas.* Written by Anne Carroll Moore. Illustrated by Jay Van Everen. (Putnam)
- *The Dream Coach.* Written by Anne Parrish. Illustrated by Anne Parrish and Dillwyn Parrish. (Macmillan)

1926—*Shen of the Sea.* Written by Arthur Bowie Chrisman. Illustrated by Else Hasselriis. (Dutton)

Honor Book:

- *The Voyagers.* Written by Padraic Colum. Illustrated by Wilfred Jones. (Macmillan)

1927—*Smoky the Cowhorse*. Written and illustrated by Will James. (Scribner)

Honor Books:

- No Record

1928—*Gay-Neck, the Story of a Pigeon*. Written by Dhan Gopal Mukerji. Illustrated by Boris Artzybasheff. (Dutton)

Honor Books:

- *The Wonder Smith and His Son*. Written by Ella Young. Illustrated by Boris Artzybasheff. (Longmans)

- *Downright Dencey*. Written by Caroline Snedeker. Illustrated by Maginel Wright Barney. (Doubleday)

1929—*The Trumpeter of Krakow*. Written by Eric P. Kelly. Illustrated by Aniela Pruszynska. (Macmillan)

Honor Books:

- *The Pigtail of Ah Lee Ben Loo*. Written and illustrated by John Bennett. (Longmans)

- *Millions of Cats*. Written and illustrated by Wanda Gág. (Coward-McCann)

- *The Boy Who Was*. Written by Grace Hallock. Illustrated by Harrie Wood. (Dutton)

- *Clearing Weather*. Written by Cornelia Meigs. Illustrated by Frank Dobias. (Little, Brown)

- *The Runaway Papoose*. Written by Grace Moon. Illustrated by Carl Moon. (Doubleday)

- *Tod of the Fens*. Written by Elinor Whitney. Illustrated by Warwick Goble. (Macmillan)

1930—*Hitty: Her First Hundred Years*. Written by Rachel Field. Illustrated by Dorothy P. Lathrop. (Macmillan)

Honor Books:

- *Daughter of the Seine*. Written by Jeanette Eaton. Illustrated with photographs. (Harper)

- *Pran of Albania*. Written by Elizabeth Miller. Illustrated by Maud Petersham and Miska Petersham. (Doubleday)

- *The Jumping-Off Place*. Written by Marian Hurd McNeely. Illustrated by William Siegel. (Longmans)

- *The Tangle-Coated Horse and Other Tales*. Written by Ella Young. Illustrated by Vera Bock. (Longmans)

- *Vaino*. Written by Julia Davis Adams. Illustrated by Lempi Ostman. (Dutton)

- *Little Blacknose*. Written by Hildegarde Swift. Illustrated by Lynd Ward. (Harcourt)

1931—*The Cat Who Went to Heaven*. Written by Elizabeth Coatsworth. Illustrated by Lynd Ward. (Macmillan)

Honor Books:

- *Floating Island*. Written and illustrated by Anne Parrish. (Harper)

- *The Dark Star of Itza*. Written by Alida Malkus. Illustrated by Lowell Houser. (Harcourt)

- *Queer Person*. Written by Ralph Hubbard. Illustrated by Harold von Schmidt. (Doubleday)

- *Mountains Are Free*. Written by Julia Davis Adams. Illustrated by Theodore Nadejen. (Dutton)

- *Spice and the Devil's Cave*. Written by Agnes Hewes. Illustrated by Lynd Ward. (Knopf)

- *Meggy MacIntosh*. Written by Elizabeth Janet Gray. Illustrated by Marguerite de Angeli. (Doubleday)

- *Garram the Hunter*. Written by Herbert Best. Illustrated by Erick Berry. (Doubleday)

- *Ood-le-uk the Wanderer.* Written by Alice Lide and Margaret Johansen. Illustrated by Raymond Lufkin. (Little, Brown)

1932—*Waterless Mountain.* Written by Laura Adams Armer. Illustrated by Sidney Armer and Laura Armer. (Longmans)

Honor Books:

- *The Fairy Circus.* Written and illustrated by Dorothy Lathrop. (Macmillan)

- *Calico Bush.* Written by Rachel Field. Illustrated by Allen Lewis. (Macmillan)

- *Boy of the South Seas.* Written by Eunice Tietjens. Illustrated by Myrtle Sheldon. (Coward-McCann)

- *Out of the Flame.* Written by Eloise Lownsbery. Illustrated by Elizabeth Tyler Wolcott. (Longmans)

- *Jane's Island.* Written by Marjorie Allee. Illustrated by Maitland De Gorgorza. (Houghton Mifflin)

- *The Truce of the Wolf and Other Tales of Old Italy.* Written by Mary Gould Davis. Illustrated by Jay Van Everen. (Harcourt)

1933—*Young Fu of the Upper Yangtze.* Written by Elizabeth Lewis. Illustrated by Kurt Wiese. (Winston)

Honor Books:

- *Swift Rivers.* Written by Cornelia Meigs. Frontispiece by Peter Hurd. (Little, Brown)

- *The Railroad to Freedom.* Written by Hildegarde Swift. Illustrated by James Daugherty. (Harcourt)

- *Children of the Soil.* Written by Nora Burglon. Illustrated by Edgar Parin d'Aulaire. (Doubleday)

1934—*Invincible Louisa.* Written by Cornelia Meigs. Illustrated with photographs. (Little, Brown)

Honor Books:

- *The Forgotten Daughter.* Written by Caroline Snedeker. (Doubleday)

- *Swords of Steel.* Written by Elsie Singmaster. Illustrated by David Hendrickson. (Houghton)

- *ABC Bunny.* Written and illustrated by Wanda Gág. (Coward-McCann)

- *The Winged Girl of Knossos.* Written and illustrated by Erik Berry [pseudonym of Allena Best]. (Appleton-Century)

- *New Land.* Written by Sarah Schmidt. Illustrated by Frank Dobias. (McBride)

- *The Big Tree of Bunlahy.* Written by Padraic Colum. Illustrated by Jack Yeats. (Macmillan)

- *Glory of the Seas.* Written by Agnes Hewes with an illustration by N. C. Wyeth. (Knopf)

- *The Apprentice of Florence.* Written by Anne Kyle. Illustrated by Erick Berry. (Houghton Mifflin)

1935—*Dobry.* Written by Monica Shannon. Illustrated by Atanas Katchamakoff. (Viking)

Honor Books:

- *The Pageant of Chinese History.* Written by Elizabeth Seeger. Illustrated by Bernard Watkins. (Longmans)

- *Davy Crockett.* Written by Constance Rourke. Illustrated by Walter Seaton. (Harcourt)

- *A Day on Skates.* Written and illustrated by Hilda van Stockum. (Harper)

1936—*Caddie Woodlawn.* Written by Carol Ryrie Brink. Illustrated by Kate Seredy. (Macmillan)

Honor Books:

- *Honk, the Moose.* Written by Phil Stong. Illustrated by Kurt Wiese. (Dodd, Mead)

- *The Good Master.* Written and illustrated by Kate Seredy. (Viking)

- *Young Walter Scott.* Written by Elizabeth Janet Gray. Jacket and endpapers by Kate Seredy. (Viking)

- *All Sail Set.* Written and illustrated by Armstrong Sperry. (Winston)

1937—*Roller Skates.* Written by Ruth Sawyer. Illustrated by Valenti Angelo. (Viking)

Honor Books:

- *Phebe Fairchild: Her Book.* Written and illustrated by Lois Lenski. (Stokes)

- *Whistlers' Van.* Written by Idwal Jones. Illustrated by Zhenya Gay. (Viking)

- *The Golden Basket.* Written and illustrated by Ludwig Bemelmans. (Viking)

- *Winterbound.* Written by Margery Bianco. Endpapers by Kate Seredy. (Viking)

- *Audubon.* Written by Constance Rourke. Illustrated by James MacDonald and James J. Audubon. (Harcourt)

- *The Codfish Musket.* Written by Agnes Hewes. Endpapers by Armstrong Sperry. (Doubleday)

1938—*The White Stag.* Written and illustrated by Kate Seredy. (Viking)

Honor Books:

- *Pecos Bill.* Written by James Cloyd Bowman. Illustrated by Laura Bannon. (Little, Brown)

- *Bright Island.* Written by Mabel Robinson. Illustrated by Lynd Ward. (Random House)

- *On the Banks of Plum Creek.* Written by Laura Ingalls Wilder. Illustrated by Garth Williams. (Harper)

1939—*Thimble Summer.* Written and illustrated by Elizabeth Enright. (Rinehart)

Honor Books:

- *Nino.* Written and illustrated by Valenti Angelo. (Viking)

- *Mr. Popper's Penguins.* Written by Richard Atwater and Florence Atwater. Illustrated by Robert Lawson. (Little, Brown)

- *"Hello the Boat!"* Written by Phyllis Crawford. (Holt)

- *Leader by Destiny: George Washington, Man and Patriot.* Written by Jeanette Eaton. Illustrated by Jack Manley Rose. (Harcourt)

- *Penn.* Written by Elizabeth Janet Gray. Illustrated by George Whitney. (Viking)

1940—*Daniel Boone.* Written and illustrated by James Daugherty. (Viking)

Honor Books:

- *The Singing Tree.* Written and illustrated by Kate Seredy. (Viking)

- *Runner of the Mountain Tops.* Written by Mabel Robinson. Illustrated by Lynd Ward. (Random House)

- *By the Shores of Silver Lake.* Written by Laura Ingalls Wilder. Illustrated by Garth Williams. (Harper)

- *Boy with a Pack.* Written by Stephen W. Meader. Illustrated by Edward Shenton. (Harcourt)

1941—*Call It Courage.* Written and illustrated by Armstrong Sperry. (Macmillan)

Honor Books:

- *Blue Willow.* Written by Doris Gates. Illustrated by Paul Lantz. (Viking)

- *Young Mac of Fort Vancouver.* Written by Mary Jane Carr. Illustrated by Richard Holberg. (Crowell)

- *The Long Winter.* Written by Laura Ingalls Wilder. Illustrated by Garth Williams. (Harper)

- *Nansen.* Written by Anna Gertrude Hall. Illustrated by Boris Artzybasheff. (Viking)

1942—*The Matchlock Gun.* Written by Walter D. Edmonds. Illustrated by Paul Lantz. (Dodd, Mead)

Honor Books:

- *Little Town on the Prairie.* Written by Laura Ingalls Wilder. Illustrated by Garth Williams. (Harper)

- *George Washington's World.* Written and illustrated by Genevieve Foster. (Scribner)

- *Indian Captive: The Story of Mary Jemison.* Written and illustrated by Lois Lenski. (Lippincott)

- *Down Ryton Water.* Written by Eva Roe Gaggin. Jacket and endpapers by Elmer Hader. (Viking)

1943—*Adam of the Road.* Written by Elizabeth Janet Gray. Illustrated by Robert Lawson. (Viking)

Honor Books:

- *The Middle Moffat.* Written by Eleanor Estes. Illustrated by Louis Slobodkin. (Harcourt)

- *Have You Seen Tom Thumb?* Written by Mabel Leigh Hunt. Illustrated by Fritz Eichenberg. (Lippincott)

1944—*Johnny Tremain.* Written by Esther Forbes. Illustrated by Lynd Ward. (Houghton Mifflin)

Honor Books:

- *These Happy Golden Years.* Written by Laura Ingalls Wilder. Illustrated by Garth Williams. (Harper)

- *Fog Magic.* Written by Julia Sauer. Endpapers by Lynd Ward. (Viking)

- *Rufus M.* Written by Eleanor Estes. Illustrated by Louis Slobodkin. (Harcourt)

- *Mountain Born.* Written by Elizabeth Yates. Illustrated by Nora S. Unwin. (Coward-McCann)

1945—*Rabbit Hill.* Written and illustrated by Robert Lawson. (Viking)

Honor Books:

- *The Hundred Dresses.* Written by Eleanor Estes. Illustrated by Louis Slobodkin. (Harcourt)

- *The Silver Pencil.* Written by Alice Dalgliesh. Illustrated by Katherine Milhouse. (Scribner)

- *Abraham Lincoln's World.* Written and illustrated by Genevieve Foster. (Scribner)

- *Lone Journey: the Life of Roger Williams.* Written by Jeanette Eaton. Illustrated by Woodi Ishmael. (Harcourt)

1946—*Strawberry Girl.* Written and illustrated by Lois Lenski. (Lippincott)

Honor Books:

- *Justin Morgan Had a Horse.* Written by Marguerite Henry. Illustrated by Wesley Dennis. (Rand McNally)

- *The Moved-Outers.* Written by Florence Crannell Means. (Houghton Mifflin)

- *Bhimsa, the Dancing Bear*. Written by Christine Weston. Illustrated by Roger Duvoisin. (Scribner)
- *New Found World*. Written by Katherine Shippen. Illustrated by C. B. Falls. (Viking)

1947—*Miss Hickory*. Written by Carolyn Bailey. Illustrated by Ruth Gannett. (Viking)

Honor Books:

- *The Wonderful Year*. Written by Nancy Barnes. Illustrated by Kate Seredy. (Messner)
- *Big Tree*. Written and illustrated by Mary Buff and Conrad Buff. (Viking)
- *The Heavenly Tenants*. Written by William Maxwell. Illustrated by Ilonka Karasz. (Harper)
- *The Avion My Uncle Flew*. Written by Cyrus Fisher [pseudonym of Darwin L. Teilhet]. Illustrated by Richard Floethe. (Appleton)
- *The Hidden Treasure of Glaston*. Written by Eleanore Jewett. Illustrated by Frederick T. Chapman. (Viking)

1948—*The Twenty-One Balloons*. Written and illustrated by William Pène du Bois. (Viking)

Honor Books:

- *Pancakes-Paris*. Written by Claire Huchet Bishop. Illustrated by Georges Schreiber. (Viking)
- *LiLun, Lad of Courage*. Written by Carolyn Treffinger. Illustrated by Kurt Wiese. (Abingdon)
- *The Quaint and Curious Quest of Johnny Longfoot*. Written by Catherine Besterman. Illustrated by Warren Chappell. (Bobbs Merrill)

- *The Cow-Tail Switch and Other West African Stories*. Written by Harold Courlander and George Herzog. Illustrated by Madye Lee Chastain. (Holt)
- *Misty of Chincoteague*. Written by Marguerite Henry. (Rand McNally)

1949—*King of the Wind*. Written by Marguerite Henry. Illustrated by Wesley Dennis (Rand McNally)

Honor Books:

- *Seabird*. Written and illustrated by Holling C. Holling. (Houghton Mifflin)
- *Daughter of the Mountains*. Written by Louise Rankin. Illustrated by Kurt Wiese. (Viking)
- *My Father's Dragon*. Written by Ruth Gannett. Illustrated by Ruth Chrisman Gannett. (Random House)
- *Story of the Negro*. Written by Arna Bontemps. (Knopf)

1950—*The Door in the Wall*. Written and illustrated by Marguerite de Angeli. (Doubleday)

Honor Books:

- *Tree of Freedom*. Written by Rebecca Caudill. Illustrated by Dorothy Bayley Morse. (Viking)
- *The Blue Cat of Castle Town*. Written by Catherine Coblentz. Illustrated by Wilfred Jones. (Longmans)
- *Kildee House*. Written by Rutherford Montgomery. Illustrated by Barbara Cooney. (Doubleday)
- *George Washington*. Written and illustrated by Genevieve Foster. (Scribner)
- *Song of the Pines*. Written by Walter Havighurst and Marion Havighurst. Illustrated by Richard Floethe. (Winston)

1951—*Amos Fortune. Free Man.* Written by Elizabeth Yates. Illustrated by Nora S. Unwin. (Aladdin)

Honor Books:

- *Better Known As Johnny Appleseed.* Written by Mabel Leigh Hunt. Illustrated by James Daugherty. (Lippincott)
- *Gandhi: Fighter Without a Sword.* Written by Jeanette Eaton. Illustrated by Ralph Ray. (Morrow)
- *Abraham Lincoln: Friend of the People.* Written by Clara Ingram Judson. Illustrated by Robert Frankenberg. (Wilcox and Follett)
- *The Story of Appleby Capple.* Written and illustrated by Anne Parrish. (Harper)

1952—*Ginger Pye.* Written and illustrated by Eleanor Estes. (Harcourt)

Honor Books:

- *Americans Before Columbus.* Written by Elizabeth Baity. Illustrated by C. B. Falls. (Viking)
- *Minn of the Mississippi.* Written and illustrated by Holling C. Holling. (Houghton Mifflin)
- *The Defender.* Written by Nicholas Kalashnikoff. Illustrated by Claire Louden and George Louden. (Scribner)
- *The Light at Tern Rock.* Written by Julia Sauer. Illustrated by Georges Schrieber. (Viking)
- *The Apple and the Arrow.* Written and illustrated by Mary Buff and Conrad Buff. (Houghton Mifflin)

1953—*Secret of the Andes.* Written by Ann Nolan Clark. Illustrated by Jean Charlot. (Viking)

Honor Books:

- *Charlotte's Web.* Written by E. B. White. Illustrated by Garth Williams. (Harper)
- *Moccasin Trail.* Written by Eloise McGraw. (Coward-McCann)
- *Red Sails to Capri.* Written by Ann Weil. Illustrated by C. B. Falls. (Viking)
- *The Bears on Hemlock Mountain.* Written by Alice Dalgliesh. Illustrated by Helen Sewell. (Scribner)
- *Birthdays of Freedom,* Vol. I. Written and illustrated by Genevieve Foster. (Scribner)

1954—*. . . And Now Miguel.* Written by Joseph Krumgold. Illustrated by Jean Charlot. (Crowell)

Honor Books:

- *All Alone.* Written by Claire Huchet Bishop. Illustrated by Feodor Rojankovsky. (Viking)
- *Shadrach.* Written by Meindert DeJong. Illustrated by Maurice Sendak. (Harper)
- *Hurry Home, Candy.* Written by Meindert DeJong. Illustrated by Maurice Sendak. (Harper)
- *Theodore Roosevelt: Fighting Patriot.* Written by Clara Ingram Judson. Illustrated by Lorence F. Bjorklund. (Follett)
- *Magic Maize.* Written and illustrated by Mary Buff and Conrad Buff. (Houghton Mifflin)

1955—*The Wheel on the School.* Written by Meindert DeJong. Illustrated by Maurice Sendak. (Harper)

Honor Books:

- *The Courage of Sarah Noble.* Written by Alice Dalgliesh. Illustrated by Leonard Weisgard. (Scribner)

- *Banner in the Sky*. Written by James Ullman. (Lippincott)

1956—*Carry On, Mr. Bowditch.* Written by Jean Lee Latham. Illustrated by John O'Hara Cosgrave, II. (Houghton Mifflin)

Honor Books:

- *The Secret River*. Written by Marjorie Kinnan Rawlings. Illustrated by Leonard Weisgard. (Scribner)
- *The Golden Name Day*. Written by Jennie Lindquist. Illustrated by Garth Williams. (Harper)
- *Men, Microscopes, and Living Things*. Written by Katherine Shippen. Illustrated by Anthony Ravielli. (Viking)

1957—*Miracles on Maple Hill.* Written by Virginia Sorensen. Illustrated by Beth Krush and Joe Krush. (Harcourt)

Honor Books:

- *Old Yeller*. Written by Fred Gipson. Illustrated by Carl Burger. (Harper)
- *The House of Sixty Fathers*. Written by Meindert DeJong. Illustrated by Maurice Sendak. (Harper)
- *Mr. Justice Holmes*. Written by Clara Ingram Judson. Illustrated by Robert Todd. (Follett)
- *The Corn Grows Ripe*. Written by Dorothy Rhoads. Illustrated by Jean Charlot. (Viking)
- *Black Fox of Lorne*. Written and illustrated by Marguerite de Angeli. (Doubleday)

1958—*Rifles for Watie.* Written by Harold Keith. (Crowell)

Honor Books:

- *The Horsecatcher*. Written by Mari Sandoz. (Westminster)

- *Gone-Away Lake*. Written by Elizabeth Enright. Illustrated by Beth Krush and Joe Krush. (Harcourt)
- *The Great Wheel*. Written and illustrated by Robert Lawson. (Viking)
- *Tom Paine: Freedom's Apostle*. Written by Leo Gurko. Illustrated by Fritz Kredel. (Crowell)

1959—*The Witch of Blackbird Pond.* Written by Elizabeth George Speare. (Houghton Mifflin)

Honor Books:

- *The Family Under the Bridge*. Written by Natalie S. Carlson. Illustrated by Garth Williams. (Harper)
- *Along Came a Dog*. Written by Meindert DeJong. Illustrated by Maurice Sendak. (Harper)
- *Chúcaro: Wild Pony of the Pampa*. Written by Francis Kalnay. Illustrated by Julian de Miskey. (Harcourt)
- *The Perilous Road*. Written by William O. Steele. Illustrated by Paul Galdone. (Harcourt)

1960—*Onion John.* Written by Joseph Krumgold. Illustrated by Symeon Shimin. (Crowell)

Honor Books:

- *My Side of the Mountain*. Written and illustrated by Jean Craighead George. (Dutton)
- *America Is Born*. Written by Gerald W. Johnson. Illustrated by Leonard Everett Fisher. (Morrow)
- *The Gammage Cup*. Written by Carol Kendall. Illustrated by Erik Blegvad. (Harcourt)

1961—*Island of the Blue Dolphins.* Written by Scott O'Dell. (Houghton Mifflin)

Honor Books:

- *America Moves Forward.* Written by Gerald W. Johnson. Illustrated by Leonard Everett Fisher. (Morrow)

- *Old Ramon.* Written by Jack Schaefer. Illustrated by Harold West. (Houghton Mifflin)

- *The Cricket in Times Square.* Written by George Selden [pseudonym of George Thompson]. Illustrated by Garth Williams. (Farrar, Straus)

1962—*The Bronze Bow.* Written by Elizabeth George Speare. (Houghton Mifflin)

Honor Books:

- *Frontier Living.* Written and illustrated by Edwin Tunis. (World)

- *The Golden Goblet.* Written by Eloise Jarvis McGraw. (Coward–McCann)

- *Belling the Tiger.* Written by Mary Stolz. Illustrated by Beni Montresor. (Harper)

1963—*A Wrinkle in Time.* Written by Madeleine L'Engle. (Farrar)

Honor Books:

- *Thistle and Thyme: Tales and Legends from Scotland.* Written by Sorche Nic Leodhas [pseudonym of Leclaire Alger]. Illustrated by Evaline Ness. (Holt)

- *Men of Athens.* Written by Olivia Coolidge. Illustrated by Milton Johnson. (Houghton Mifflin)

1964—*It's Like This, Cat.* Written by Emily Neville. Illustrated by Emil Weiss. (Harper)

Honor Books:

- *Rascal.* Written by Sterling North. Illustrated by John Schoenherr. (Dutton)

- *The Loner.* Written by Ester Wier. Illustrated by Christine Price. (McKay)

1965—*Shadow of a Bull.* Written by Maia Wojciechowska. Illustrated by Alvin Smith. (Atheneum)

Honor Book:

- *Across Five Aprils.* Written by Irene Hunt. (Follett)

1966—*I, Juan de Pareja.* Written by Elizabeth Borton de Treviño. (Farrar)

Honor Books:

- *The Animal Family.* Written by Randall Jarrell. Illustrated by Maurice Sendak. (Pantheon)

- *The Black Cauldron.* Written by Lloyd Alexander. (Holt)

- *The Noonday Friends.* Written by Mary Stolz. Illustrated by Louis S. Glanzman. (Harper)

1967—*Up a Road Slowly.* Written by Irene Hunt. (Follett)

Honor Books:

- *The Jazz Man.* Written by Mary Hays Weik. Illustrated by Ann Grifalconi. (Atheneum)

- *The King's Fifth.* Written by Scott O'Dell. Illustrated by Samuel Bryant. (Houghton Mifflin)

- *Zlateh the Goat and Other Stories.* Written by Isaac Bashevis Singer. Illustrated by Maurice Sendak. (Harper)

1968—*From the Mixed-up Files of Mrs. Basil E. Frankweiler.* Written and illustrated by E. L. Konigsburg. (Atheneum)

Honor Books:

- *Jennifer, Hecate, Macbeth, William McKinley, and Me, Elizabeth.* Written and illustrated by E. L. Konigsburg. (Atheneum)

- *The Black Pearl.* Written by Scott O'Dell. (Houghton Mifflin)
- *The Egypt Game.* Written by Zilpha Keatley Snyder. Illustrated by Alton Raible. (Atheneum)
- *The Fearsome Inn.* Written by Isaac Bashevis Singer. Illustrated by Nonny Hogrogian. (Scribner)

1969—*The High King.* Written by Lloyd Alexander. (Holt)

Honor Books:

- *To Be a Slave.* Written by Julius Lester. Illustrated by Tom Feelings. (Dial)
- *When Shlemiel Went to Warsaw and Other Stories.* Written by Isaac Bashevis Singer. Illustrated by Margot Zemach. (Farrar, Straus)

1970—*Sounder.* Written by William H. Armstrong. Illustrated by James Barkley. (Harper)

Honor Books:

- *The Journey Outside.* Written by Mary Q. Steele. Illustrated by Rocco Negri. (Viking)
- *Our Eddie.* Written by Sulamith Ish-Kishor. (Pantheon)
- *The Many Ways of Seeing: An Introduction to the Pleasures of Art.* Written by Janet Gaylord Moore. Various artists. (World)

1971—*The Summer of the Swans.* Written by Betsy Byars. Illustrated by Ted CoConis. (Viking)

Honor Books:

- *Enchantress from the Stars.* Written by Sylvia Louise Engdahl. Illustrated by Rodney Shackell. (Atheneum)
- *Kneeknock Rise.* Written and illustrated by Natalie Babbitt. (Farrar, Straus)

- *Sing Down the Moon.* Written by Scott O'Dell. (Houghton Mifflin)

1972—*Mrs. Frisby and the Rats of NIMH.* Written by Robert C. O'Brien [pseudonym of Robert Leslie Conly]. Illustrated by Zena Bernstein. (Atheneum)

Honor Books:

- *Annie and the Old One.* Written by Miska Miles. Illustrated by Peter Parnall. (Atlantic–Little)
- *Incident at Hawk's Hill.* Written by Allan W. Eckert. Illustrated by John Schoenherr. (Little, Brown)
- *The Headless Cupid.* Written by Zilpha Keatley Snyder. Illustrated by Alton Raible. (Atheneum)
- *The Planet of Junior Brown.* Written by Virginia Hamilton. (Macmillan)
- *The Tombs of Atuan.* Written by Ursula K. LeGuin. Illustrated by Gail Garraty. (Atheneum)

1973—*Julie of the Wolves.* Written by Jean Craighead George. Illustrated by John Schoenherr. (Harper)

Honor Books:

- *Frog and Toad Together.* Written and illustrated by Arnold Lobel. (Harper)
- *The Upstairs Room.* Written by Johanna Reiss. (Crowell)
- *The Witches of Worm.* Written by Zilpha Keatley Snyder. Illustrated by Alton Raible. (Atheneum)

1974—*The Slave Dancer.* Written by Paula Fox. Illustrated by Eros Keith. (Bradbury)

Honor Book:

- *The Dark Is Rising.* Written by Susan Cooper. Illustrated by Alan E. Cober. (Atheneum/McElderry)

1975—*M. C. Higgins, the Great.* Written by Virginia Hamilton. (Macmillan)

Honor Books:

- *Figgs and Phantoms.* Written and illustrated by Ellen Raskin. (Dutton)

- *My Brother Sam Is Dead.* Written by James Lincoln Collier and Christopher Collier. (Four Winds)

- *Philip Hall Likes Me. I Reckon Maybe.* Written by Bette Greene. Illustrated by Charles Lilley. (Dial)

- *The Perilous Gard.* Written by Elizabeth Marie Pope. Illustrated by Richard Cuffari. (Houghton Mifflin)

1976—*The Grey King.* Written by Susan Cooper. Illustrated by Michael Heslop. (Atheneum)

Honor Books:

- *The Hundred Penny Box.* Written by Sharon Bell Mathis. Illustrated by Leo Dillon and Diane Dillon. (Viking)

- *Dragonwings.* Written by Laurence Yep. (Harper)

1977—*Roll of Thunder, Hear My Cry.* Written by Mildred Taylor. (Dial)

Honor Books:

- *A String in the Harp.* Written by Nancy Bond. (Atheneum/McElderry)

- *Abel's Island.* Written and illustrated by William Steig. (Farrar)

1978—*Bridge to Terabithia.* Written by Katherine Paterson. Illustrated by Donna Diamond. (Crowell)

Honor Books:

- *Ramona and Her Father.* Written by Beverly Cleary. Illustrated by Alan Tiegreen. (Morrow)

- *Anpao: An American Indian Odyssey.* Written by Jamake Highwater. Illustrated by Fritz Scholder. (Lippincott)

1979—*The Westing Game.* Written and illustrated by Ellen Raskin. (Dutton)

Honor Book:

- *The Great Gilly Hopkins.* Written by Katherine Paterson. (Crowell)

1980—*A Gathering of Days: A New England Girl's Journal 1830-32.* Written by Joan W. Blos. (Scribner)

Honor Book:

- *The Road From Home: The Story of an Armenian Girl.* Written by David Kherdian. (Greenwillow)

1981—*Jacob Have I Loved.* Written by Katherine Paterson. (Crowell)

Honor Books:

- *The Fledgling.* Written by Jane Langton. (Harper)

- *A Ring of Endless Light.* Written by Madeleine L'Engle. (Farrar)

1982—*A Visit to William Blake's Inn.* Written by Nancy Willard. Illustrated by Alice Provensen and Martin Provensen. (Harcourt)

Honor Books:

- *Ramona Quimby, Age 8.* Written by Beverly Cleary. Illustrated by Alan Tiegreen. (Morrow)

- *Upon the Head of the Goat: A Childhood in Hungary, 1939-1944.* Written by Aranka Siegal. (Farrar)

1983—*Dicey's Song.* Written by Cynthia Voigt. (Atheneum)

Honor Books:

- *Graven Images*. Written by Paul Fleischman. Illustrated by Andrew Glass. (Harper)
- *Homesick: My Own Story*. Written by Jean Fritz. Illustrated by Margot Tomes. (Putnam)
- *Sweet Whispers, Brother Rush*. Written by Virginia Hamilton. (Philomel)
- *The Blue Sword*. Written by Robin McKinley. (Greenwillow)
- *Doctor De Soto*. Written and illustrated by William Steig. (Farrar)

1984—*Dear Mr. Henshaw*. Written by Beverly Cleary. Illustrated by Paul O. Zelinsky. (Morrow)

Honor Books:

- *The Wish Giver*. Written by Bill Brittain. Illustrated by Andrew Glass. (Harper)
- *Sugaring Time*. Written by Kathryn Lasky. Photographs by Christopher G. Knight. (Macmillan)
- *The Sign of the Beaver*. Written by Elizabeth George Speare. (Houghton)
- *A Solitary Blue*. Written by Cynthia Voigt. (Atheneum)

1985—*The Hero and the Crown*. Written by Robin McKinley. (Greenwillow)

Honor Books:

- *The Moves Make the Man*. Written by Bruce Brooks. (Harper)
- *One-Eyed Cat*. Written by Paula Fox. (Bradbury)
- *Like Jake and Me*. Written by Mavis Jukes. Illustrated by Lloyd Bloom. (Knopf)

1986—*Sarah, Plain and Tall*. Written by Patricia MacLachlan. (Harper)

Honor Books:

- *Commodore Perry in the Land of the Shogun*. Written and illustrated by Rhoda Blumberg. (Lothrop)
- *Dogsong*. Written by Gary Paulsen. (Bradbury)

1987—*The Whipping Boy*. Written by Sid Fleischman. Illustrated by Peter Sis. (Greenwillow)

Honor Books:

- *On My Honor*. Written by Marion Dane Bauer. (Clarion)
- *A Fine White Dust*. Written by Cynthia Rylant. (Bradbury)
- *Volcano: The Eruption and Healing of Mount St. Helens*. Written by Patricia Lauber. Photographs by various artists. (Bradbury)

1988—*Lincoln: A Photobiography*. Written by Russell Freedman. Illustrated with photographs. (Clarion)

Honor Books:

- *Hatchet*. Written by Gary Paulsen. (Bradbury)
- *After the Rain*. Written by Norma Fox Mazer. (Morrow)

1989—*Joyful Noise: Poems for Two Voices*. Written by Paul Fleischman. Illustrated by Eric Beddows. (Harper)

Honor Books:

- *Scorpions*. Written by Walter Dean Myers. (Harper)
- *In the Beginning*. Written by Virginia Hamilton. Illustrated by Barry Moser. (Harcourt)

1990—*Number the Stars*. Written by Lois Lowry. (Houghton Mifflin)

Honor Books:

- *Afternoon of the Elves.* Written by Janet Taylor Lisle. (Orchard)
- *Shabanu: Daughter of the Wind.* Written by Suzanne Fisher Staples. (Knopf)
- *The Winter Room.* Written by Gary Paulsen. (Orchard)

1991—*Maniac Magee.* Written by Jerry Spinelli. (Little, Brown)

Honor Book:

- *The True Confessions of Charlotte Doyle.* Written by Avi. Illustrated by Ruth E. Murray. (Orchard)

1992—*Shiloh.* Written by Phyllis Reynolds Naylor. (Atheneum)

Honor Books:

- *Nothing But the Truth.* Written by Avi. (Orchard)
- *The Wright Brothers.* Written by Russell Freedman. Photographs by Wilbur Wright and Orville Wright. (Holt)

1993—*Missing May.* Written by Cynthia Rylant. (Orchard)

Honor Books:

- *The Dark-Thirty: Southern Tales of the Supernatural.* Written by Patricia McKissack. Illustrated by Brian Pinkney. (Knopf)
- *Somewhere in the Darkness.* Written by Walter Dean Myers. (Scholastic)
- *What Hearts.* Written by Bruce Brooks. (HarperCollins)

1994—*The Giver.* Written by Lois Lowry. (Houghton Mifflin)

Honor Books:

- *Crazy Lady!* Written by Jane Leslie Conly. (HarperCollins)

- *Dragon's Gate.* Written by Laurence Yep. (HarperCollins)
- *Eleanor Roosevelt: A Life of Discovery.* Written by Russell Freedman. Photographs by various artists. (Clarion)

1995—*Walk Two Moons.* Written by Sharon Creech. (HarperCollins)

Honor Books:

- *Catherine, Called Birdy.* Written by Karen Cushman. (Clarion)
- *The Ear, the Eye and the Arm.* Written by Nancy Farmer. (Orchard)

1996—*The Midwife's Apprentice.* Written by Karen Cushman. (Clarion)

Honor Books:

- *What Jamie Saw.* Written by Carolyn Coman. (Front Street)
- *The Watsons Go to Birmingham—1963.* Written by Christopher Paul Curtis. (Delacorte)
- *Yolonda's Genius.* Written by Carol Fenner. (Margaret McElderry)
- *The Great Fire.* Written by Jim Murphy. Photographs by various artisits. (Scholastic)

1997—*The View from Saturday.* Written by E. L. Konigsburg. (Atheneum)

Honor Books:

- *A Girl Named Disaster.* Written by Nancy Farmer. (Orchard)
- *The Moorchild.* Written by Eloise McGraw. (Margaret McElderry)
- *The Thief.* Written by Megan Whalen Turner. (Greenwillow)
- *Belle Prater's Boy.* Written by Ruth White. (Farrar)

1998—*Out of the Dust.* Written by Karen Hesse. (Scholastic)

Honor Books:

- *Lily's Crossing.* Written by Patricia Reilly Giff. (Delacorte)
- *Ella Enchanted.* Written by Gail Carson Levine. (HarperCollins)
- *Wringer.* Written by Jerry Spinelli. (HarperCollins)

1999—*Holes.* Written by Louis Sachar. (Farrar)

Honor Book:

- *A Long Way From Chicago.* Written by Richard Peck. (Dial)

2000—*Bud, Not Buddy.* Written by Christopher Paul Curtis. (Delacorte)

Honor Books:

- *Getting Near to Baby.* Written by Audrey Couloumbis. (Putnam)
- *Our Only May Amelia.* Written by Jennifer L. Holm. Photographs by various artists. (HarperCollins)
- *26 Fairmount Avenue.* Written and illustrated by Tomie dePaola. (Putnam)

THE CALDECOTT MEDAL WINNERS

1938—*Animals of the Bible.* Illustrated by Dorothy P. Lathrop. Text selected by Helen Dean Fish. (Lippincott)

Honor Books:

- *Seven Simeons: A Russian Tale.* Illustrated and retold by Boris Artzybasheff. (Viking)
- *Four and Twenty Blackbirds . . . .* Illustrated by Robert Lawson. Compiled by Helen Dean Fish. (Stokes)

1939—*Mei Li.* Illustrated and written by Thomas Handforth. (Doubleday)

Honor Books:

- *The Forest Pool.* Illustrated and written by Laura Adams Armer. (Longmans)
- *Wee Gillis.* Illustrated by Robert Lawson. Written by Munro Leaf. (Viking)
- *Snow White and the Seven Dwarfs.* Illustrated and translated by Wanda Gág. (Coward-McCann)
- *Barkis.* Illustrated and written by Clare Turlay Newberry. (Harper)
- *Andy and the Lion.* Illustrated and written by James Daugherty. (Viking)

1940—*Abraham Lincoln.* Illustrated and written by Ingri d'Aulaire and Edgar Parin d'Aulaire. (Doubleday)

Honor Books:

- *Cock-a Doodle Doo . . . .* Illustrated and written by Berta Hader and Elmer Hader. (Macmillan)
- *Madeline.* Illustrated and written by Ludwig Bemelmans. (Viking)
- *The Ageless Story.* Illustrated by Lauren Ford. Text excerpted from the Bible. (Dodd Mead)

1941—*They Were Strong and Good.* Illustrated and written by Robert Lawson. (Viking)

Honor Book:

- *April's Kittens.* Illustrated and written by Clare Turlay Newberry. (Harper)

1942—*Make Way for Ducklings.* Illustrated and written by Robert McCloskey. (Viking)

Honor Books:

- *An American ABC.* Illustrated and written by Maud Petersham and Miska Petersham. (Macmillan)
- *In My Mother's House.* Illustrated by Velino Herrera. Written by Ann Nolan Clark. (Viking)
- *Paddle-to-the-Sea.* Illustrated and written by Holling C. Holling. (Houghton Mifflin)

- *Nothing at All.* Illustrated and written by Wanda Gág. (Coward-McCann)

1943—*The Little House.* Illustrated and written by Virginia Lee Burton. (Houghton Mifflin)

Honor Books:

- *Dash and Dart.* Illustrated and written by Mary Buff and Conrad Buff. (Viking)
- *Marshmallow.* Illustrated and written by Clare Turlay Newberry. (Harper)

1944—*Many Moons.* Illustrated by Louis Slobodkin. Written by James Thurber. (Harcourt)

Honor Books:

- *Small Rain: Verses from the Bible.* Illustrated by Elizabeth Orton Jones. Verses selected by Jessie Orton Jones. (Viking)
- *Pierre Pidgeon.* Illustrated by Arnold E. Bare. Written by Lee Kingman. (Houghton Mifflin)
- *The Mighty Hunter.* Illustrated and written by Berta Hader and Elmer Hader. (Macmillan)
- *A Child's Good Night Book.* Illustrated by Jean Charlot. Written by Margaret Wise Brown. (W. R. Scott)
- *The Good-Luck Horse.* Illustrated by Plato Chan. Written by Chih-Yi Chan. (Whittlesey)

1945—*Prayer for a Child.* Illustrated by Elizabeth Orton Jones. Written by Rachel Field. (Macmillan)

Honor Books:

- *Mother Goose.* Illustrated and verses selected by Tasha Tudor. (Walck)
- *In the Forest.* Illustrated and written by Marie Hall Ets. (Viking)

- *Yonie Wondernose.* Illustrated and written by Marguerite de Angeli. (Doubleday)
- *The Christmas Anna Angel.* Illustrated by Kate Seredy. Written by Ruth Sawyer. (Viking)

1946—*The Rooster Crows . . . .* Illustrated and text selected by Maud Petersham and Miska Petersham. (Macmillan)

Honor Books:

- *Little Lost Lamb.* Illustrated by Leonard Weisgard. Written by Golden MacDonald [pseudonym of Margaret Wise Brown]. (Doubleday)
- *Sing Mother Goose.* Illustrated by Marjorie Torrey. Music by Opal Wheeler. (Dutton)
- *My Mother Is the Most Beautiful Woman in the World.* Illustrated by Ruth Gannett. Retold by Becky Reyher. (Lothrop)
- *You Can Write Chinese.* Illustrated and written by Kurt Wiese. (Viking)

1947—*The Little Island.* Illustrated by Leonard Weisgard. Written by Golden MacDonald [pseudonym of Margaret Wise Brown]. (Doubleday)

Honor Books:

- *Rain Drop Splash.* Illustrated by Leonard Weisgard. Written by Alvin Tresselt. (Lothrop)
- *The Boats on the River.* Illustrated by Jay Hyde Barnum. Written by Marjorie Flack. (Viking)
- *Timothy Turtle.* Illustrated by Tony Palazzo. Written by Al Graham. (Robert Welsh Publishing)
- *Pedro, the Angel of Olvera Street.* Illustrated and written by Leo Politi. (Scribner)

- *Sing in Praise: A Collection of the Best-Loved Hymns.* Illustrated by Marjorie Torrey. Stories of hymns and music arranged by Opal Wheeler. (Dutton)

1948—*White Snow, Bright Snow.* Illustrated by Roger Duvoisin. Written by Alvin Tresselt. (Lothrop)

Honor Books:

- *Stone Soup.* Illustrated and written by Marcia Brown. (Scribner)

- *McElligot's Pool.* Illustrated and written by Dr. Seuss [pseudonym of Theodor Seuss Geisel]. (Random House)

- *Bambino the Clown.* Illustrated and written by George Schreiber. (Viking)

- *Roger and the Fox.* Illustrated by Hildegard Woodward. Written by Lavinia R. Davis. (Doubleday)

- *Song of Robin Hood.* Designed and illustrated by Virginia Lee Burton. Selected and edited by Anne Malcolmson. (Houghton Mifflin)

1949—*The Big Snow.* Illustrated and written by Berta Hader and Elmer Hader. (Macmillan)

Honor Books:

- *Blueberries for Sal.* Illustrated and written by Robert McCloskey. (Viking)

- *All Around the Town.* Illustrated by Helen Stone. Written by Phyllis McGinley. (Lippincott)

- *Juanita.* Illustrated and written by Leo Politi. (Scribner)

- *Fish in the Air.* Illustrated and written by Kurt Wiese. (Viking)

1950—*Song of the Swallows.* Illustrated and written by Leo Politi. (Scribner)

Honor Books:

- *America's Ethan Allen.* Illustrated by Lynd Ward. Written by Stewart Holbrook. (Houghton Mifflin)

- *The Wild Birthday Cake.* Illustrated by Hildegard Woodward. Written by Lavinia R. Davis. (Doubleday)

- *The Happy Day.* Illustrated by Marc Simont. Written by Ruth Krauss. (Harper)

- *Bartholomew and the Oobleck.* Illustrated and written by Dr. Seuss [pseudonym of Theodor Seuss Geisel]. (Random House)

- *Henry-Fisherman.* Illustrated and written by Marcia Brown. (Scribner)

1951—*The Egg Tree.* Illustrated and written by Katherine Milhous. (Scribner)

Honor Books:

- *Dick Whittington and His Cat.* Illustrated and written by Marcia Brown. (Scribner)

- *The Two Reds.* Illustrated by Nicolas [pseudonym of Nicolas Mordvinoff]. Written by Will [pseudonym of William Lipkind]. (Harcourt)

- *If I Ran the Zoo.* Illustrated and written by Dr. Seuss [pseudonym of Theodor Seuss Geisel]. (Random House)

- *The Most Wonderful Doll in the World.* Illustrated by Helen Stone. Written by Phyllis McGinley. (Lippincott)

- *T-Bone, the Baby-Sitter.* Illustrated and written by Clare Turlay Newberry. (Harper)

1952—*Finders Keepers.* Illustrated by Nicolas [pseudonym of Nicolas Mordvinoff]. Written by Will [pseudonym of William Lipkind]. (Harcourt)

Honor Books:

- *Mr. T. W. Anthony Woo.* Illustrated and written by Marie Hall Ets. (Viking)

- *Skipper John's Cook.* Illustrated and written by Marcia Brown. (Scribner)

- *All Falling Down*. Illustrated by Margaret Bloy Graham. Written by Gene Zion. (Harper)

- *Bear Party*. Illustrated and written by William Pène du Bois. (Viking)

- *Feather Mountain*. Illustrated and written by Elizabeth Olds. (Houghton Mifflin)

1953—*The Biggest Bear*. Illustrated and written by Lynd Ward. (Houghton Mifflin)

Honor Books:

- *Puss in Boots*. Illustrated and translated by Marcia Brown. (Scribner)

- *One Morning in Maine*. Illustrated and written by Robert McCloskey. (Viking)

- *Ape in a Cape: An Alphabet of Odd Animals*. Illustrated and written by Fritz Eichenberg. (Harcourt)

- *The Storm Book*. Illustrated by Margaret Bloy Graham. Written by Charlotte Zolotow. (Harper)

- *Five Little Monkeys*. Illustrated and written by Juliet Kepes. (Houghton Mifflin)

1954—*Madeline's Rescue*. Illustrated and written by Ludwig Bemelmans. (Viking)

Honor Books:

- *Journey Cake, Ho!* Illustrated by Robert McCloskey. Written by Ruth Sawyer. (Viking)

- *When Will the World Be Mine?* Illustrated by Jean Charlot. Written by Miriam Schlein. (W. R. Scott)

- *The Steadfast Tin Soldier*. Illustrated by Marcia Brown. Translated by M. R. James. (Scribner)

- *A Very Special House*. Illustrated by Maurice Sendak. Written by Ruth Krauss. (Harper)

- *Green Eyes*. Illustrated and written by A. Birnbaum. (Capitol)

1955—*Cinderella, or the Little Glass Slipper*. Illustrated and translated from Charles Perrault by Marcia Brown. (Scribner)

Honor Books:

- *Book of Nursery and Mother Goose Rhymes*. Illustrated and text selected by Marguerite de Angeli. (Doubleday)

- *Wheel on the Chimney*. Illustrated by Tibor Gergely. Written by Margaret Wise Brown. (Lippincott)

- *The Thanksgiving Story*. Illustrated by Helen Sewell. Written by Alice Dalgliesh. (Scribner)

1956—*Frog Went A-Courtin'*. Illustrated by Feodor Rojankovsky. Retold by John Langstaff. (Harcourt)

Honor Books:

- *Play With Me*. Illustrated and written by Marie Hall Ets. (Viking)

- *Crow Boy*. Illustrated and written by Taro Yashima. (Viking)

1957—*A Tree Is Nice*. Illustrated by Marc Simont. Written by Janice May Udry. (Harper)

Honor Books:

- *Mr. Penny's Race Horse*. Illustrated and written by Marie Hall Ets. (Viking)

- *1 Is One*. Illustrated and written by Tasha Tudor. (Walck)

- *Anatole*. Illustrated by Paul Galdone. Written by Eve Titus. (McGraw-Hill)

- *Gillespie and the Guards*. Illustrated by James Daugherty. Written by Benjamin Elkin. (Viking)

- *Lion*. Illustrated and written by William Pène du Bois. (Viking)

1958—*Time of Wonder*. Illustrated and written by Robert McCloskey. (Viking)

Honor Books:

- *Fly High, Fly Low*. Illustrated and written by Don Freeman. (Viking)

- *Anatole and the Cat*. Illustrated by Paul Galdone. Written by Eve Titus. (McGraw–Hill)

1959—*Chanticleer and the Fox*. Illustrated and adapted from Chaucer's *Canterbury Tales* by Barbara Cooney. (Crowell)

Honor Books:

- *The House That Jack Built: La Maison Que Jacques A Batie*. Illustrated and written by Antonio Frasconi. (Harcourt)

- *What Do You Say, Dear?* Illustrated by Maurice Sendak. Written by Sesyle Joslin. (W. R. Scott)

- *Umbrella*. Illustrated and written by Taro Yashima. (Viking)

1960—*Nine Days to Christmas*. Illustrated by Marie Hall Ets. Written by Marie Hall Ets and Aurora Labastida. (Viking)

Honor Books:

- *Houses from the Sea*. Illustrated by Adrienne Adams. Written by Alice E. Goudey. (Scribner)

- *The Moon Jumpers*. Illustrated by Maurice Sendak. Written by Janice May Udry. (Harper)

1961—*Baboushka and the Three Kings*. Illustrated by Nicholas Sidjakov. Written by Ruth Robbins. (Parnassus Press)

Honor Book:

- *Inch by Inch*. Illustrated and written by Leo Lionni. (Ivan Obolensky)

1962—*Once a Mouse*. Illustrated and retold by Marcia Brown. (Scribner)

Honor Books:

- *The Fox Went Out on a Chilly Night: An Old Song*. Illustrated by Peter Spier. (Doubleday)

- *Little Bear's Visit*. Illustrated by Maurice Sendak. Written by Else Holmelund Minarik. (Harper)

- *The Day We Saw the Sun Come Up*. Illustrated by Adrienne Adams. Written by Alice E. Goudey. (Scribner)

1963—*The Snowy Day*. Illustrated and written by Ezra Jack Keats. (Viking)

Honor Books:

- *The Sun Is a Golden Earring*. Illustrated by Bernarda Bryson. Written by Natalia M. Belting. (Holt)

- *Mr. Rabbit and the Lovely Present*. Illustrated by Maurice Sendak. Written by Charlotte Zolotow. (Harper)

1964—*Where the Wild Things Are*. Illustrated and written by Maurice Sendak. (Harper)

Honor Books:

- *Swimmy*. Illustrated and written by Leo Lionni. (Pantheon)

- *All in the Morning Early*. Illustrated by Evaline Ness. Written by Sorche Nic Leodhas [pseudonym of Leclaire Alger]. (Holt)

- *Mother Goose and Nursery Rhymes*. Illustrated and text selected by Philip Reed. (Atheneum)

1965—*May I Bring a Friend?* Illustrated by Beni Montresor. Written by Beatrice Schenk de Regniers. (Atheneum)

Honor Books:

- *Rain Makes Applesauce*. Illustrated by Marvin Bileck. Written by Julian Scheer. (Holiday House)

- *The Wave*. Illustrated by Blair Lent. Written by Margaret Hodges. (Houghton Mifflin)
- *A Pocketful of Cricket*. Illustrated by Evaline Ness. Written by Rebecca Caudill. (Holt)

1966—*Always Room for One More*. Illustrated by Nonny Hogrogian. Adapted by Sorche Nic Leodhas [pseudonym of Leclaire Alger]. (Holt)

Honor Books:

- *Hide and Seek Fog*. Illustrated by Roger Duvoisin. Written by Alvin Tresselt. (Lothrop)
- *Just Me*. Illustrated by Marie Hall Ets. (Viking)
- *Tom Tit Tot*. Illustrated by Evaline Ness. Written by Joseph Jacobs. (Scribner)

1967—*Sam, Bangs and Moonshine*. Illustrated and written by Evaline Ness. (Holt)

Honor Book:

- *One Wide River to Cross*. Illustrated by Ed Emberley. Written by Barbara Emberley. (Prentice-Hall)

1968—*Drummer Hoff*. Illustrated by Ed Emberley. Adapted by Barbara Emberley. (Prentice-Hall)

Honor Books:

- *Seashore Story*. Illustrated and written by Taro Yashima. (Viking)
- *Frederick*. Illustrated and written by Leo Lionni. (Pantheon)
- *The Emperor and the Kite*. Illustrated by Ed Young. Written by Jane Yolen. (World)

1969—*The Fool of the World and the Flying Ship*. Illustrated by Uri Shulevitz. Retold by Arthur Ransome. (Farrar)

Honor Book:

- *Why the Sun and the Moon Live in the Sky: An African Folktale*. Illustrated by Blair Lent. Written by Elphinstone Dayrell. (Houghton Mifflin)

1970—*Sylvester and the Magic Pebble*. Illustrated and written by William Steig. (Windmill Books)

Honor Books:

- *Alexander and the Wind-up Mouse*. Illustrated and written by Leo Lionni. (Pantheon)
- *Goggles!* Illustrated and written by Ezra Jack Keats. (Macmillan)
- *Pop Corn & Ma Goodness*. Illustrated by Robert Andrew Parker. Written by Edna Mitchell Preston. (Viking)
- *The Judge: An Untrue Tale*. Illustrated by Margot Zemach. Written by Harve Zemach. (Farrar, Straus)
- *Thy Friend, Obadiah*. Illustrated and written by Brinton Turkle. (Viking)

1971—*A Story, A Story*. Illustrated and retold by Gail E. Haley. (Atheneum)

Honor Books:

- *The Angry Moon*. Illustrated by Blair Lent. Retold by William Sleator. (Atlantic Little)
- *Frog and Toad Are Friends*. Illustrated and written by Arnold Lobel. (Harper)
- *In the Night Kitchen*. Illustrated and written by Maurice Sendak. (Harper)

1972—*One Fine Day*. Illustrated and adapted by Nonny Hogrogian. (Macmillan)

Honor Books:

- *Hildilid's Night*. Illustrated by Arnold Lobel. Written by Cheli Durán Ryan. (Macmillan)

- *If All the Seas Were One Sea.* Illustrated and written by Janina Domanska. (Macmillan)
- *Moja Means One: Swahili Counting Book.* Illustrated by Tom Feelings. Written by Muriel Feelings. (Dial)

1973—*The Funny Little Woman.* Illustrated by Blair Lent. Retold by Arlene Mosel. (Dutton)

Honor Books:

- *Hosie's Alphabet.* Illustrated by Leonard Baskin. Written by Hosea, Tobias, and Lisa Baskin. (Viking)
- *Snow-White and the Seven Dwarfs.* Illustrated by Nancy Ekholm Burkert. Translated by Randall Jarrell. (Farrar, Straus)
- *When Clay Sings.* Illustrated by Tom Bahti. Written by Byrd Baylor. (Scribner)
- *Anansi the Spider.* Illustrated and written by Gerald McDermott. (Holt)

1974—*Duffy and the Devil.* Illustrated by Margot Zemach. Retold by Harve Zemach. (Farrar)

Honor Books:

- *Cathedral: The Story of Its Construction.* Illustrated and written by David Macaulay. (Houghton Mifflin)
- *The Three Jovial Huntsmen.* Illustrated and written by Susan Jeffers. (Bradbury)

1975—*Arrow to the Sun.* Illustrated and retold by Gerald McDermott. (Viking)

Honor Book:

- *Jambo Means Hello: A Swahili Alphabet Book.* Illustrated by Tom Feelings. Written by Muriel Feelings. (Dial)

1976—*Why Mosquitoes Buzz in People's Ears.* Illustrated by Leo Dillon and Diane Dillon. Retold by Verna Aardema. (Dial)

Honor Books:

- *Strega Nona.* Illustrated and retold by Tomie de Paola. (Prentice-Hall)
- *The Desert Is Theirs.* Illustrated by Peter Parnall. Written by Byrd Baylor. (Scribner)

1977—*Ashanti to Zulu: African Traditions.* Illustrated by Leo Dillon and Diane Dillon. Written by Margaret Musgrove. (Dial)

Honor Books:

- *The Amazing Bone.* Illustrated and written by William Steig. (Farrar)
- *The Contest.* Illustrated and adapted by Nonny Hogrogian. (Greenwillow)
- *Fish for Supper.* Illustrated and written by M. B. Goffstein. (Dial)
- *The Golem: A Jewish Legend.* Illustrated and retold by Beverly Brodsky McDermott. (Lippincott)
- *Hawk, I'm Your Brother.* Illustrated by Peter Parnall. Written by Byrd Baylor. (Scribner)

1978—*Noah's Ark.* Illustrated and translated by Peter Spier. (Doubleday)

Honor Books:

- *Castle.* Illustrated and written by David Macaulay. (Houghton)
- *It Could Always Be Worse.* Illustrated and retold by Margot Zemach. (Farrar)

1979—*The Girl Who Loved Wild Horses.* Illustrated and written by Paul Goble. (Bradbury)

Honor Books:

- *Freight Train.* Illustrated and written by Donald Crews. (Greenwillow)
- *The Way to Start a Day.* Illustrated by Peter Parnall. Written by Byrd Baylor. (Scribner)

1980—*Ox-Cart Man.* Illustrated by Barbara Cooney. Written by Donald Hall. (Viking)

Honor Books:

- *Ben's Trumpet.* Illustrated and written by Rachel Isadora. (Greenwillow)
- *The Garden of Abdul Gasazi.* Illustrated and written by Chris Van Allsburg. (Houghton Mifflin)
- *The Treasure.* Illustrated and retold by Uri Shulevitz. (Farrar)

1981—*Fables.* Illustrated and written by Arnold Lobel. (Harper)

Honor Books:

- *The Grey Lady and the Strawberry Snatcher.* Illustrated and conceived by Molly Bang. (Four Winds)
- *The Bremen-Town Musicians.* Illustrated and retold by Ilse Plume. (Doubleday)
- *Mice Twice.* Illustrated and written by Joseph Low. (Atheneum/McElderry)
- *Truck.* Illustrated and written by Donald Crews. (Greenwillow)

1982—*Jumanji.* Illustrated and written by Chris Van Allsburg. (Houghton Mifflin)

Honor Books:

- *On Market Street.* Illustrated by Anita Lobel. Written by Arnold Lobel. (Greenwillow)
- *Outside Over There.* Illustrated and written by Maurice Sendak. (Harper)
- *A Visit to William Blake's Inn: Poems for Innocent and Experienced Travelers.* Illustrated by Alice Provensen and Martin Provensen. Written by Nancy Willard. (Harcourt)
- *Where the Buffaloes Begin.* Illustrated by Stephen Gammell. Written by Olaf Baker. (Warne)

1983—*Shadow.* Illustrated and translated by Marcia Brown. (Scribner)

Honor Books:

- *A Chair for My Mother.* Illustrated and written by Vera B. Williams. (Greenwillow)
- *When I Was Young in the Mountains.* Illustrated by Diane Goode. Written by Cynthia Rylant. (Dutton)

1984—*The Glorious Flight: Across the Channel With Louis Blériot July 25, 1919.* Illustrated and written by Alice Provensen and Martin Provensen. (Viking)

Honor Books:

- *Little Red Riding Hood.* Illustrated and retold by Trina Schart Hyman. (Holiday House)
- *Ten, Nine, Eight.* Illustrated and written by Molly Bang. (Greenwillow)

1985—*Saint George and the Dragon.* Illustrated by Trina Schart Hyman. Retold by Margaret Hodges. (Little, Brown)

Honor Books:

- *Hansel and Gretel.* Illustrated by Paul O. Zelinsky. Retold by Rika Lesser. (Dodd)
- *Have You Seen My Duckling?* Illustrated and written by Nancy Tafuri. (Greenwillow)
- *The Story of Jumping Mouse.* Illustrated and written by John Steptoe. (Lothrop)

1986—*The Polar Express.* Illustrated and written by Chris Van Allsburg. (Houghton Mifflin)

Honor Books:

- *King Bidgood's in the Bathtub.* Illustrated by Don Wood. Written by Audrey Wood. (Harcourt)

- *The Relatives Came*. Illustrated by Stephen Gammell. Written by Cynthia Rylant. (Bradbury)

1987—*Hey, Al!* Illustrated by Richard Egielski. Written by Arthur Yorinks. (Farrar)

Honor Books:

- *Rumplestiltskin*. Illustrated and written by Paul O. Zelinsky. (Dodd)
- *The Village of Round and Square Houses*. Illustrated and written by Ann Grifalconi. (Little, Brown)
- *Alphabatics*. Illustrated by Suse MacDonald. (Bradbury)

1988—*Owl Moon*. Illustrated by John Schoenherr. Written by Jane Yolen. (Philomel Books)

Honor Book:

- *Mufaro's Beautiful Daughters*. Illustrated and written by John Steptoe. (Lothrop)

1989—*Song and Dance Man*. Illustrated by Stephen Gammell. Written by Karen Ackerman. (Knopf)

Honor Books:

- *Mirandy and Brother Wind*. Illustrated by Jerry Pinkney. Written by Patricia C. McKissack. (Knopf)
- *Free Fall*. Illustrated and conceived by David Wiesner. (Lothrop)
- *The Boy of the Three-Year Nap*. Illustrated by Allen Say. Retold by Dianne Snyder. (Houghton Mifflin)
- *Goldilocks and the Three Bears*. Illustrated and retold by James Marshall. (Dial)

1990—*Lon Po Po: A Red-Riding Hood Story from China*. Illustrated and translated by Ed Young. (Philomel)

Honor Books:

- *Bill Peet: An Autobiography*. Illustrated and written by Bill Peet. (Houghton Mifflin)
- *The Talking Eggs*. Illustrated by Jerry Pinkney. Written by Robert D. San Souci. (Dial)
- *Hershel and the Hanukkah Goblins*. Illustrated by Trina Schart Hyman. Written by Eric Kimmel. (Holiday House)
- *Color Zoo*. Illustrated and written by Lois Ehlert. (Lippincott)

1991—*Black and White*. Illustrated and written by David Macaulay. (Houghton Mifflin)

Honor Books:

- *Puss in Boots*. Illustrated by Fred Marcellino. Translated by Malcolm Arthur. (Farrar)
- *"More More More," Said the Baby*. Illustrated and written by Vera B. Williams. (Greenwillow)

1992—*Tuesday*. Illustrated and written by David Wiesner. (Clarion)

Honor Book:

- *Tar Beach*. Illustrated and written by Faith Ringgold. (Crown)

1993—*Mirette on the High Wire*. Illustrated and written by Emily Arnold McCully. (Putnam)

Honor Books:

- *Seven Blind Mice*. Illustrated and retold by Ed Young. (Philomel)
- *The Stinky Cheese Man and Other Fairly Stupid Tales*. Illustrated by Lane Smith. Written by Jon Scieszka. (Viking)
- *Working Cotton*. Illustrated by Carole Byard. Written by Sherley Ann Williams. (Harcourt)

1994—*Grandfather's Journey.* Illustrated and written by Allen Say. (Houghton Mifflin)

Honor Books:

- *In the Small, Small Pond.* Illustrated and written by Denise Fleming. (Holt)
- *Owen.* Illustrated and written by Kevin Henkes. (Greenwillow)
- *Peppe the Lamplighter.* Illustrated by Ted Lewin. Written by Elisa Bartone. (Lothrop)
- *Raven: A Trickster Tale from the Pacific Northwest.* Illustrated and retold by Gerald McDermott. (Harcourt)
- *Yo! Yes?* Illustrated and written by Chris Raschka. (Orchard)

1995—*Smoky Night.* Illustrated by David Diaz. Written by Eve Bunting. (Harcourt Brace)

Honor Books:

- *Swamp Angel.* Illustrated by Paul O. Zelinsky. Written by Anne Isaacs. (Dutton)
- *John Henry.* Illustrated by Jerry Pinkney. Written by Julius Lester. (Dial)
- *Time Flies.* Illustrated and conceived by Eric Rohmann. (Crown)

1996—*Officer Buckle and Gloria.* Illustrated and written by Peggy Rathmann. (Putnam)

Honor Books:

- *Alphabet City.* Illustrated and conceived by Stephen P. Johnson. (Viking)
- *Zin! Zin! Zin! A Violin.* Illustrated by Marjorie Priceman. Written by Lloyd Moss. (Simon and Schuster)
- *The Faithful Friend.* Illustrated by Brian Pinkney. Retold by Robert D. San Souci. (Simon and Schuster)
- *Tops and Bottoms.* Illustrated and retold by Janet Stevens. (Harcourt)

1997—*Golem.* Illustrated and retold by David Wisniewski. (Clarion)

Honor Books:

- *Hush!: A Thai Lullaby.* Illustrated by Holly Meade. Written by Minfong Ho. (Orchard)
- *The Graphic Alphabet.* Illustrated and conceived by David Pelletier. (Orchard)
- *The Paperboy.* Illustrated and written by Dav Pilkey. (Orchard)
- *Starry Messenger: Galileo Galilei.* Illustrated and written by Peter Sis. (Farrar)

1998—*Rapunzel.* Illustrated and retold by Paul O. Zelinsky. (Dutton)

Honor Books:

- *Harlem.* Illustrated by Christopher Myers. Written by Walter Dean Myers. (Scholastic)
- *The Gardener.* Illustrated by David Small. Written by Sara Stewart. (Farrar)
- *There Was an Old Lady Who Swallowed a Fly.* Illustrated and retold by Simms Taback. (Viking)

1999—*Snowflake Bentley.* Illustrated by Mary Azarian. Written by Jacqueline Briggs Martin. (Houghton Mifflin)

Honor Books:

- *Duke Ellington.* Illustrated by Brian Pinkney. Written by Andrea Davis Pinkney. (Hyperion)
- *No, David!* Illustrated and written by David Shannon. (Scholastic)
- *Snow.* Illustrated and written by Uri Shulevitz. (Farrar)
- *Tibet: Through the Red Box.* Illustrated and written by Peter Sis. (Farrar)

2000—*Joseph Had a Little Overcoat.* Illustrated and written by Simms Taback. (Viking)

Honor Books:

- *A Child's Calendar*. Illustrated by Trina Schart Hyman. Written by John Updike. (Holiday House)

- *Sector 7*. Illustrated and written by David Weisner. (Clarion)

- *When Sophie Gets Angry—Really, Really Angry*. Illustrated and written by Molly Bang. (Scholastic)

- *The Ugly Duckling*. Illustrated and adapted by Jerry Pinkney. Original text by Hans Christian Andersen. (Morrow)

REFERENCES

Allen, Terry J. "Mary Azarian." *The Horn Book Magazine* (July/August 1999): 430–33.

Avi. "The True Confessions of Charlotte Doyle." *The Horn Book Magazine* (January/February 1992): 24–27.

Azarian, Mary. "Caldecott Medal Acceptance." *The Horn Book Magazine* (July/August 1999): 423–29.

Babbitt, Natalie. "Patricia MacLachlan: The Biography." *The Horn Book Magazine* (July/August 1986): 414–16.

Bader, Barbara. *American Picture Books from Noah's Ark to the Beast Within.* New York: Macmillan, 1976.

Billington, Elizabeth T. *The Randolph Caldecott Treasury.* New York: Frederick Warne & Company, 1978.

Bowen, Brenda. "Karen Hesse." *The Horn Book Magazine* (July/August 1998): 428–32.

Brooks, Donna. "Paul O. Zelinsky: Geishas on Tractors." *The Horn Book Magazine* (July/August 1998): 442–49.

Carpenter, Humphrey, and Mari Prichard. *The Oxford Companion to Children's Literature.* Oxford, England: Oxford University Press, 1974.

Carroll, Lewis. *The Annotated Alice: Alice's Adventures in Wonderland and Through the Looking Glass.* With an introduction and notes by Martin Gardner. New York: Bramhall House, 1960.

Cohen, Morton N., ed. *The Selected Letters of Lewis Carroll.* New York: Pantheon Books, 1978.

Commire, Anne. Something About the Author Series. Vols. 1–7, 11, 12, 14, 18–20, 24, 29, 33, 37, 40, 47, 49, 50, 60, 64, 66, 68–71, 73–76, 78–80, 83, 86, 89, 91, 92, 95, 96. Detroit: Gale Research Company, 1971–98.

Cott, Jonathan. *Pipers at the Gates of Dawn: The Wisdom of Children's Literature.* New York: Random House, 1983.

Crawford, Bartholow V., Alexander C. Kern, and Morriss H. Needleman. *American Literature.* New York: Barnes and Noble, 1953.

Creech, Sharon. "Newbery Medal Acceptance." *The Horn Book Magazine* (July/August 1995): 418–25.

Cummings, Pat. *Talking with Artists.* New York: Bradbury Press, 1992.

———. *Talking with Artists Volume II.* New York: Bradbury Press, 1995.

Cushman, Karen. "Newbery Medal Acceptance." *The Horn Book Magazine* (July/August 1996): 413–19.

Cushman, Philip. "Karen Cushman." *The Horn Book Magazine* (July/August 1996): 420–23.

Davis, Mary Gould. "Helen Dean Fish 1889–1953." *The Horn Book Magazine* (April 1953): 89.

———. *Randolph Caldecott: An Appreciation.* Philadelphia: J. B. Lippincott, 1946.

Dawson, Mitchell. "Genevieve Foster's Worlds." *The Horn Book Magazine* (June 1952): 190–95.

Deitch, Gene. "Filming 'Zlateh the Goat.' " *The Horn Book Magazine* (June 1975): 241–49.

DeMontreville, Doris, and Elizabeth D. Crawford. *Fourth Book of Junior Authors and Illustrators.* New York: H. W. Wilson, 1978.

DeMontreville, Doris, and Donna Hill. *Third Book of Junior Authors.* New York: H. W. Wilson, 1972.

Dempsey, Frank J. "Russell Freedman." *The Horn Book Magazine* (July/August 1988): 452–56.

Diaz, Cecelia. "David Diaz." *The Horn Book Magazine.* (July/August 1995): 434–35.

Diaz, David. "Caldecott Medal Acceptance." *The Horn Book Magazine* (July/August 1995): 430–33.

Donaldson, Elizabeth, and Gerald. *The Book of Days.* New York: A & W, 1979.

Doyle, Brian. *The Who's Who of Children's Literature.* New York: Schocken Books, 1968.

Egielski, Richard. "Caldecott Medal Acceptance." *The Horn Book Magazine* (July/August 1987): 433–35.

Elledge, Scott. *E. B. White: A Biography.* New York: W. W. Norton and Company, 1984.

Engen, Rodney K. *Randolph Caldecott: "Lord of the Nursery."* London: Bloomsbury Books, 1976.

Evans, Dilys. "David Wisniewski." *The Horn Book Magazine* (July/August 1997): 424–26.

Field, Elinor Whitney. *Horn Book Reflections.* Boston: The Horn Book, 1969.

Fleischman, Paul. "Newbery Medal Acceptance." *The Horn Book Magazine* (July/August 1989): 442–51.

Fleischman, Sid. "Newbery Medal Acceptance." *The Horn Book Magazine* (July/August 1987): 423–28.

———. "Paul Fleischman." *The Horn Book Magazine* (July/August 1989): 452–55.

Freedman, Russell. "Eleanor Roosevelt: A Life of Discovery." *The Horn Book Magazine* (January/February 1995): 33–36.

———. "Newbery Medal Acceptance." *The Horn Book Magazine* (July/August 1988): 444–51.

Fuller, Muriel. *More Junior Authors.* New York: H. W. Wilson, 1963.

Galbraith, Lachlan N. "Marjorie Kinnan Rawlings' *The Secret River.*" *Elementary English* (April 1975): 455–59.

Gauch, Patricia Lee. "Ed Young." *The Horn Book Magazine* (July/August 1990): 430–35.

———. "John Schoenherr," *The Horn Book Magazine* (July/August 1988): 460–63.

Gregory, Ruth W. *Special Days.* Secaucus, NJ: The Citadel Press, 1978.

Guth, Dorothy Lobrano, ed. *Letters of E. B. White.* New York: Harper and Row, 1976.

Hackett, Alice Payne. *60 Years of Best Sellers 1895–1955.* New York: R. R. Bowker, 1956.

Haley-James, Shirley. "Lois Lowry." *The Horn Book Magazine* (July/August 1990): 422–24.

Harrison, Barbara, and Gregory Maguire, eds. *Innocence and Experience: Essays and Conversations on Children's Literature.* New York: Lothrop, Lee & Shepard, 1987.

Haviland, Virginia. *Children's Literature: Views and Reviews.* Glenview, IL: Scott, Foresman, 1973.

Hearn, Michael Patrick. "Maurice Sendak." *Riverbank Review* (Summer 1999): 10–13.

Hendrickson, Robert. *The Literary Life and Other Curiosities.* New York: Harcourt Brace, 1994.

Hepperman, Christine. "Meindert DeJong." *Riverbank Review* (Winter 1998/1999): 18–20.

Hesse, Karen. "Newbery Medal Acceptance." *The Horn Book Magazine* (July/August 1998): 422–27.

Higgins, James E. "Kate Seredy: Storyteller." *The Horn Book Magazine* (April 1968): 162–68.

Hodges, Jack. *The Genius of Writers.* New York: St. Martin's Press, 1994.

Holtze, Sally Holmes. *Fifth Book of Junior Authors and Illustrators.* New York: H. W. Wilson, 1983.

——. "A Second Look: *The Animal Family.*" *The Horn Book Magazine* (November/December 1985): 714–16.

——. *Seventh Book of Junior Authors and Illustrators.* New York: H. W. Wilson, 1996.

——. *Sixth Book of Junior Authors and Illustrators.* New York: H. W. Wilson, 1989.

Izard, Anne R. "Newbery and Caldecott Awards 1959." *ALA Bulletin* (April 1959): 309–10.

Jones, Neal T., ed. *A Book of Days for the Literary Year.* New York: Thames and Hudson, 1984.

Kassen, Aileen. "Kate Seredy: A Person Worth Knowing." *Elementary English* (March 1968): 303–15.

Keats, Ezra Jack. "Dear Mr. Keats." *The Horn Book Magazine* (June 1972): 306–10.

Keller, John. "Jerry Spinelli." *The Horn Book Magazine* (July/August 1991): 433–36.

Kingman, Lee. *Newbery and Caldecott Medal Books 1956–1965.* Boston: Horn Book, 1965.

——. *Newbery and Caldecott Medal Books 1966–1975.* Boston: Horn Book, 1975.

——. *Newbery and Caldecott Medal Books 1976–1985.* Boston: Horn Book, 1985.

Kingman, Lee, Joanna Foster, and Ruth Giles Lontoft. *Illustrators of Children's Books 1957–1966.* Boston: Horn Book, 1968.

Kingman, Lee, Grace Allen Hogarth, and Harriet Quimby. *Illustrators of Children's Books 1967–1976.* Boston: Horn Book, 1978.

Kirkpatrick, D. L. *Twentieth Century Children's Writers.* New York: St. Martin's Press, 1978.

——. *Twentieth Century Children's Writers,* 2d ed. New York: St. Martin's Press, 1983.

Konigsburg, E. L. "Newbery Medal Acceptance." *The Horn Book Magazine* (July/August 1997): 404–14.

Kunitz, Stanley J. *Twentieth Century Authors* (first supplement). New York: H. W. Wilson, 1955.

Kunitz, Stanley J., and Howard Haycraft. *The Junior Book of Authors,* 2d ed. New York: H. W. Wilson, 1951.

Lanes, Selma G. *The Art of Maurice Sendak.* New York: Abradale Press/Harry N. Abrams, 1980.

Lass, Abraham, ed. *A Student's Guide to 50 British Novels*. New York: Washington Square Press, 1966.

Lester, Julius. "John Henry." *The Horn Book Magazine* (January/February 1996): 28–31.

Levine, Arthur. "Emily Arnold McCully." *The Horn Book Magazine* (July/August 1993): 430–32.

Livsey, Rosemary. "Leo Politi, Friend of All." *The Horn Book Magazine* (March/April 1949): 97–108.

Lorraine, Walter. "Lois Lowry." *The Horn Book Magazine* (July/August 1994): 423–26.

Lowry, Lois. "Newbery Medal Acceptance." *The Horn Book Magazine* (July/August 1990): 412–21.

——. "Newbery Medal Acceptance." *The Horn Book Magazine* (July/August 1994): 414–22.

Macaulay, David. "Caldecott Medal Acceptance." *The Horn Book Magazine* (July/August 1991): 410–21.

——. "Chris Van Allsburg." *The Horn Book Magazine* (July/August 1986): 425–29.

——. "David Wiesner." *The Horn Book Magazine* (July/August 1992): 423–28.

McCauley, May Carole. "Life of Multitalented Silverstein Little Known." *Star Tribune* (Minneapolis). 15 May 1999, 4(E).

McCully, Emily Arnold. "Caldecott Medal Acceptance." *The Horn Book Magazine* (July/August 1993): 424–29.

McKissack, Frederick, and Patricia McKissack. "How to Write a Children's Book." *Highlights Foundation 1998 Report*, pp. 25–26.

MacLachlan, Patricia. "Newbery Medal Acceptance." *The Horn Book Magazine* (July/August 1986): 407–13.

MacLachlan, Robert. "A Hypothetical Dilemma." *The Horn Book Magazine* (July/August 1986): 416–19.

Mahoney, Bertha E., and Elinor Whitney. *Contemporary Illustrators of Children's Books*. Boston: The Bookshop for Boys and Girls, 1930.

Mahoney, Bertha E., Louise Payton Latimer, and Beula Folmsbee. *Illustrators of Children's Books 1744–1945*. Boston: Horn Book, 1947.

Marcus, Leonard S. *A Caldecott Celebration: Six Artists and Their Paths to the Caldecott Medal*. New York: Walker, 1998.

——. "An Interview with Margaret K. McElderry—Part II." *The Horn Book Magazine* (January/February 1994): 34–45.

——. *Margaret Wise Brown: Awakened by the Moon*. Boston: Beacon Press, 1992.

——. "Rearrangement of Memory: An Interview with Allen Say." *The Horn Book Magazine*. (May/June 1991): 295–303.

Meigs, Cornelia. *Invincible Louisa*. Boston: Little, Brown, 1933.

Miller, Bertha Mahoney, and Elinor Whitney Field. *Caldecott Medal Books 1938–1957*. Boston: Horn Book, 1957.

Naylor, Phyllis Reynolds. "Newbery Medal Acceptance." *The Horn Book Magazine* (July/August 1992): 404–11.

Naylor, Rex. "Phyllis Reynolds Naylor." *The Horn Book Magazine*. (July/August 1992): 412–15.

Nelson, Randy F. *The Almanac of American Letters*. Los Altos, CA: William Kaufmann, 1981.

Neumeyer, Peter F. "The Creation of *Charlotte's Web*: From Drafts to Book Part I." *The Horn Book Magazine* (October 1982): 489–97.

———. "The Creation of *Charlotte's Web*: From Drafts to Book—Part II." *The Horn Book Magazine* (December 1982): 617–25.

Parsons, Nicholas. *The Book of Literary Lists.* New York: The Leisure Circle, 1985.

Preiss, Byron, ed. *The Art of Leo and Diane Dillon.* New York: Ballantine Books, 1981.

Rathmann, Peggy. "Caldecott Medal Acceptance." *The Horn Book Magazine* (July/August 1996): 424–27.

Rathmann–Noonan, Robin. "Aunt Peggy." *The Horn Book Magazine* (July/August 1996): 428–29.

Rigg, Lyle D. "Sharon Creech." *The Horn Book Magazine* (July/August 1995): 426–29.

Roginski, Jim. *Behind the Covers.* Englewood, CO: Libraries Unlimited, 1985.

Rylant, Cynthia. "Missing May." *The Horn Book Magazine* (January/February 1993): 52–53.

———. "Newbery Medal Acceptance." *The Horn Book Magazine* (July/August 1993): 416–19.

Sachar, Louis. "Newbery Medal Acceptance." *The Horn Book Magazine* (July/August 1999): 410–17.

Sadler, Glenn Edward. "Maurice Sendak and Dr. Seuss: A Conversation." *The Horn Book Magazine* (September/October 1989): 582–88.

Say, Allen. "Caldecott Medal Acceptance." *The Horn Book Magazine* (July/August 1994): 427–31.

———. "Grandfather's Journey." *The Horn Book Magazine* (January/February 1995): 30–32.

Say, Yuriko. "My Father." *The Horn Book Magazine* (July/August 1994): 432–35.

Scherman, David E., and Rosemarie Redlich. *Literary America.* New York: Dodd, Mead, 1952.

Schoenherr, John. "Caldecott Medal Acceptance." *The Horn Book Magazine* (July/August 1988): 457–59.

Schwartz, Anne. "Stephen Gammell." *The Horn Book Magazine* (July/August 1989): 456–59.

Shoreman, Daniel J. *Learning Through Literature: Newbery Award Winners.* Greensboro, NC: The Education Center, 1994.

Silvey, Anita, ed. *Children's Books and Their Creators.* Boston: Houghton Mifflin Company, 1968.

Silvey, Anita. "An Interview with Cynthia Rylant." *The Horn Book Magazine* (November/December 1987): 695–702.

Smaridge, Norah. *Famous Literary Teams for Young People.* New York: Dodd, Mead, 1977.

Smith, Irene. *A History of the Newbery and Caldecott Medals.* New York: Viking Press, 1957.

Smith, Lane. "The Artist at Work." *The Horn Book Magazine* (January/February 1993): 64–70.

Snyder, Dianne. "The Boy of the Three–Year Nap." *The Horn Book Magazine* (March/April 1989): 176–78.

Spinelli, Jerry. "Newbery Medal Acceptance." *The Horn Book Magazine* (July/August 1991): 426–32.

Sutherland, James, ed. *The Oxford Book of Literary Anecdotes.* Oxford, England: Oxford University Press, 1975.

Sutherland, Zena, and May Hill Arbuthnot. *Children and Books*, 5th edition. Glenview, IL: Scott, Foresman, 1977.

Tafuri, Nancy. "The Artist at Work." *The Horn Book Magazine* (November/December 1989): 732–35.

Todd, Laurie Konigsburg. "E. L. Konigsburg." *The Horn Book Magazine* (July/August 1997): 415–17.

Twain, Mark. *Adventures of Huckleberry Finn.* With an introduction by Justin Kaplan and a foreword and addendum by Victor Doyno. New York: Random House, 1996.

Van Allsburg, Chris. "Caldecott Medal Acceptance." *The Horn Book Magazine* (July/August 1986): 420–24.

———. "David Macaulay: The Early Years." *The Horn Book Magazine* (July/August 1991): 422–25.

Van Loon, Gerard Willem. *The Story of Hendrik Willem Van Loon.* Philadelphia: J. B. Lippincott, 1972.

Viguers, Ruth Hill, Marcia Dalphin, and Bertha Mahoney Miller. *Illustrators of Children's Books 1946–1956.* Boston: Horn Book, 1958.

Ward, Diane. "Cynthia Rylant." *The Horn Book Magazine* (July/August 1993): 420–23.

Ward, Martha E., and Dorothy A. Marquardt. *Authors of Books for Young People.* Metuchen, NJ: Scarecrow Press, 1967.

———. *Illustrators of Books for Young People,* 2d ed. Metuchen, NJ: Scarecrow Press, 1975.

Wiesner, David. "Caldecott Medal Acceptance." *The Horn Book Magazine* (July/August 1992): 416–22.

Wisniewski, David. "Caldecott Medal Acceptance." *The Horn Book Magazine* (July/August 1997): 418–23.

Woolman, Bertha, and Patricia Litsey. *The Caldecott Award.* Minneapolis: T. S. Denison, 1988.

———. *The Newbery Award.* Minneapolis: T. S. Denison, 1988.

Yates, Elizabeth. *Spanning Time: A Diary Keeper Becomes a Writer.* Peterborough, NH: Cobblestone, 1996.

Young, Ed. "Caldecott Medal Acceptance." *The Horn Book Magazine* (July/August 1990): 425–29.

Zelinsky, Paul O. "Caldecott Medal Acceptance." *The Horn Book Magazine* (July/August 1998): 433–41.

Zinsser, William, ed. *Worlds of Childhood: The Art and Craft of Writing for Children.* Boston: Houghton Mifflin, 1990.

Zolotow, Charlotte, and Patricia MacLachlan. "Dialogue Between Charlotte Zolotow and Patricia MacLachlan." *The Horn Book Magazine* (November/December 1989): 736–45.

NAME INDEX

This index includes authors, illustrators, editors, and others who appear in the trivia facts, including, for example, such people as Alice Liddell, on whom Lewis Carroll based the "Alice" books. For a complete list of Newbery and Caldecott recipients, please consult this book's appendixes.

TITLE INDEX

This index includes books, stories, periodicals, songs, and movies. In the case of such series books as the Hardy Boys or Beverly Cleary's books about Ramona, specific titles, when mentioned, are included as well as the name of the series. When such title characters as Huck Finn are included in an item of trivia without the complete book title, the entry is still included under the title (*Adventures of Huckleberry Finn*).

THROUGH **LIBRARIES UNLIMITED**

CALDECOTT CONNECTIONS...*Three Volumes*
Shan Glandon

In these three volumes the author demonstrates how to use award-winning books as springboards to science, social studies, and language arts learning in the library and classroom. You will also expand student awareness and appreciation of top illustrators and illustration techniques. **Grades PreK–4.**
Language Arts: xvii, 232p. 8½x11 paper ISBN 1-56308-846-0
Science: xviii, 228p. 8½x11 paper ISBN 1-56308-687-5
Social Studies: xviii, 156p. 8½x11 paper ISBN 1-56308-845-2

CORETTA SCOTT KING AWARD BOOKS: Using Great Literature with Children and Young Adults
Claire Gatrell Stephens

During the past 30 years, the titles recognized by the Coretta Scott King Award have consistently presented excellent writing, storytelling, history, and values. Access these amazing books through annotated bibliographies and a multitude of activities based on specific titles. Helpful tips and reproducibles make this a classroom-friendly resource. **Grades 3–8.**
xvi, 234p. 8½x11 paper ISBN 1-56308-685-9

CHILDREN'S BOOK AWARDS ANNUAL 1999
Matt Berman and Marigny J. Dupuy

This affordable annual guide to award-winning children's books keeps you abreast of the best in children's literature. You'll find reviews of all major national awards— Newbery, Caldecott, Coretta Scott King, Batchelder, Pura Belpre, *Boston Globe*–Horn Book, and the National Book Awards—in addition to titles listed as ALA Notables, BCCB Blue Ribbons, *Booklist* Editor's Choice, and many other honors. **Grades K–12.**
ix, 130p. 8½x11 paper ISBN 1-56308-771-5

THE NEWBERY COMPANION: Booktalk and Related Materials for Newbery Medal and Honor Books, 2d Edition
John T. Gillespie and Corinne J. Naden

A wealth of information about Newbery Award winners and honor books is at your fingertips with this new release. You'll find detailed plot summaries, booktalks, updated information about the winning titles and authors, suggestions for read-alikes, and ideas for how to introduce the books to young readers.
ca.460p. 7x10 cloth ISBN 1-56308-813-4

LET'S CELEBRATE TODAY: Calendars, Events, and Holidays
Diana F. Marks

Following a calendar format, this book lists historic events, literary achievements, famous firsts, inventions, birthdays, holidays from around the world, and more. At least three entry-related learning activities are given for each day. Use it as a daily activity guide, rainy day resource, idea source for the bulletin board or as a great way to awaken student interest in high-achievers or award-winners whose contributions have withstood the test of time. **Grades K–12.**
xvi, 337p. 8½x11 paper ISBN 1-56308-558-5

For a free catalog or to place an order, please contact Libraries Unlimited.
•Phone: 800-237-6124 • Fax: 303-220-8843 • Visit: www.lu.com
•Mail to: Dept. B041 • P.O. Box 6633 • Englewood, CO 80155-6633